The New Fostering Standards, Regulations and Statutory Guidance (England):
What's new?
What's changed?

NICK DUNSTER

Published by
British Association for Adoption & Fostering
(BAAF)
Saffron House
6-10 Kirby Street
London EC1N 8TS
www.baaf.org.uk

Charity registration 275689 (England and Wales) and SC039337 (Scotland)

© BAAF, 2011

British Library Cataloguing in Publication Data
A catalogue record for this book is available from the British Library

ISBN 978 1 907585 19 7

Project management by Shaila Shah, Director of Publications, BAAF
Designed and typeset by Helen Joubert Design
Printed in Great Britain by the Lavenham Press
Trade distribution by Turnaround Publisher Services, Unit 3, Olympia Trading Estate, Coburg Road, London N22 6TZ

BAAF is the leading UK-wide membership organisation for all those concerned with adoption, fostering and child care issues.

Contents

Acknowledgements

The value that an introductory guide of this sort has rests in part upon the speed with which it can be produced. This urgency has placed several people under considerable pressure, so I am immensely grateful to Shaila Shah and Jo Francis in BAAF for responding with such good humour and professionalism to my numerous and increasingly pesky requests for advice and assistance. I'm also indebted to David Holmes for his careful reading of early drafts at a time when there were many other pressing demands upon his time. Finally, I would like to thank Jacob, Martha and Clara for their ongoing patience: writing this guide in recent weeks has resulted in me falling some way short of the descriptions of a good, reasonable or responsible parent set out in the new standards and statutory guidance.

Note about the author

Nick Dunster is the Regional Director for BAAF (Central England). After initially studying music, he qualified as a social worker in 1993 and has since managed family placement and residential services in the statutory and voluntary sectors. He joined BAAF in 2009.

INTRODUCTION
Why now?

The arrival of a new set of fostering regulations, standards and statutory guidance provides an opportunity to take stock. What's happened since the last standards were issued? And what do the new set of standards tell us about the state of fostering in England today?

The last decade has seen some interesting patterns and themes emerge in foster care in England. The *proportion* of children in foster care has grown, rising from two-thirds of children in care ten years ago to nearly three-quarters now. Building upon the ongoing professionalisation of fostering, the *complexity* of children deemed appropriate for foster care has also increased. Foster carers now take on tasks once regarded as the preserve of the residential sector: the recent growth in parent with child placements is one example of this trend; the pilots of multi-dimensional treatment foster care another.

The commissioning and delivery of fostering provision has altered greatly since the last National Minimum Standards were issued. The rapid growth of the independent sector, particularly in the last five years, has been mirrored by renewed efforts to improve the strategic commissioning of services by local authorities, most notably in the new statutory guidance relating to sufficiency.

Few aspects of a foster child's identity have been left unaddressed by statutory guidance since the last standards were issued. The new care planning regulations and associated guidance are only the most recent waves of a great tide of initiatives seeking to improve outcomes for children in care. Statutory guidance has been published regarding, for example, children going missing, their education, their health, how best to promote their independence, and how best to protect them. *Working Together to Safeguard Children* (DCSF, 2010), the core document underpinning safeguarding and child protection, has recently been revised and expanded. All of these documents have had an impact upon fostering provision, and their extent and range have started to leave the 2002 standards and regulations behind.

An ongoing focus on corporate parenting sought to deliver all these national initiatives in ways that paid careful attention to the voice of the individual child. But the more we listened to children and young people, the more obvious it became that the scale and nature of the required changes to fostering left the 2002 standards looking procedural and cumbersome, no longer fit for purpose. A new set of standards, regulations and guidance was needed to take account of all the initiatives since 2002 and to improve outcomes for fostered children in the future.

Although many working within fostering will recognise the need for revised standards, regulations and statutory guidance, their arrival comes at a time when the sector is under considerable strain. This explains the rationale for this guide, which has been written with the following aims.

- To provide a succinct outline of the key themes running through the new regulations, standards and statutory guidance.

- To provide a comparative analysis of the old and the new standards and regulations, in sufficient detail to guide amendments to current practice where needed.

- To assist fostering services to begin the processes of self-audit and initial action planning.

The documents underpinning this guide

This guide is based upon the following documents:

- Fostering Services (England) Regulations 2011

- Fostering Services: National Minimum Standards (2011)

- Children Act Guidance and Regulations Volume 4: Fostering Services (2011)
- Fostering Services National Minimum Standards (2002)
- Fostering Services Regulations (2002)

Please note that this introductory guide is intended to highlight rather than debate the most significant changes.

A note on the structure of the guide

Chapter 1 sets out three important new themes running through the new regulations, standards and statutory guidance.

Chapter 2 consists of two tables setting out a detailed comparative analysis of the 2002 and 2011 standards and regulations. Chapter 2 contains the full text of the 2011 standards and quotations from the key changes of the 2011 regulations.

Chapter 3 is an action planning format, aiming to assist fostering services by drawing together requirements that are addressed in different places across the standards, guidance and regulations. The right hand column is left blank for notes and self-auditing.

This introductory guide has been published as soon as possible after the launch of the new standards and related documents with the primary aim of assisting fostering services. For further advice and support from BAAF, please contact your local regional office or visit our website at www.baaf.org.uk.

CHAPTER 1
So what's new?

The new statutory guidance for fostering services sets out its underpinning principles and values at the outset, all of which are consistent with other recently issued statutory guidance. The origins of these principles can be traced back to the core concepts of welfare, planning and partnership enshrined in the 1989 Children Act.

It would, however, be a mistake to regard the new fostering standards, regulations and statutory guidance as simply more of the same. There are some fundamental and significant shifts in approach running through this new set of documents.

The most significant new themes can be summarised as follows.

1. The foster carer as a parental figure

2. The child as an active agent of change

3. The importance of relationships

1 The foster carer as a parental figure

Although both the 2002 and 2011 regulations for fostering services have clung to the term foster *parent*, the rest of the fostering world has tended to distance itself from its use, fearing perhaps that it might compromise professionalisation or confuse notions of parental responsibility. Foster *carer* has been our term of choice for some time.

Over the last couple of decades, fostering professionals, with strong support from primary legislation, have spent a lot of time and energy explaining to prospective foster carers that they should never seek to replace the child's parents and that parental responsibility is always retained by the birth parent.

The new fostering standards and related statutory guidance could be said to mark the return of the foster carer as a parental figure. This does not mean, it should be emphasised, that the foster carer usurps the role of the birth parent. But it does mean that the new standards expect us to empower foster carers to take on parenting tasks on a day-to-day basis.

The good parent

Underpinning this new emphasis on the foster carer as a parental figure is the notion of the "good parent". The "good parent" yardstick is returned to repeatedly in the statutory guidance, highlighted in the quotations below for ease of reference.

Regarding medication

'Arrangements should be in line with those that any good parent *would make, taking account of the individual needs and capacity of the child.'*
(Statutory guidance paragraph 3.60)

Regarding the promotion of positive behaviour

'The policy should make it clear that physical restraint should only be used in exceptional circumstances where it is the only appropriate means to prevent likely injury to the child or other people, or likely serious damage to property, and in a manner consistent with the actions of any good parent.*'*
(Statutory guidance paragraph 3.98)

Standard 3.5   Foster carers respect the child's privacy and confidentiality, in a manner that is consistent with *good parenting*.

Regarding overnight stays

'Foster carers should always have contact details for the household in which the child will be staying. They should also make contact with the household beforehand, as would any good parent, to assist in assessing the request and to confirm arrangements…'
(Statutory guidance paragraph 3.21)

Regarding preparation for independence

'When they do leave the foster home for greater independence, it will usually be appropriate for the foster carer to remain in contact with the young person for a period of time and to offer appropriate support, as would a good parent.*'*
(Statutory guidance paragraph 3.124)

The reasonable or responsible parent

The notion of a good parent is further described and explained elsewhere in the standards. Terms such as "reasonable" and "responsible" refine the definition.

Regarding exercising choice

Standard 2.4   Children exercise choice in the food that they eat, and are able to prepare their own meals and snacks, within the context of the foster family's decision making and the limits that a *responsible parent* would set.

Standard 2.5   Children exercise choice and independence in the clothes and personal requisites that they buy and have these needs met, within the context of the foster family's decision making and the reasonable limits that a *responsible parent* would set.

Regarding leisure activities

Standard 7.5   Children have permission to take part in age appropriate peer activities as would normally be granted by a *reasonable parent* to their children, within the framework of the placement plan. Decision-making and any assessment of risk to the child should be undertaken on the same basis as a *reasonable parent* would do.

The delegation of decision making to the foster carer

Closely linked to the expectation that foster carers act in the manner of good, responsible or reasonable parents is the delegation of decision making. This is an issue returned to again and again in the statutory guidance and the standards.

There are two strands in the approach taken to the delegation of decision making:

- clarity regarding day-to-day decision making delegated to foster carers;
- increased delegation of decision making to foster carers.

Clarity regarding day-to-day decision making delegated to foster carers

The new guidance and standards see the care plan and placement plan as the key means of achieving clarity regarding decision making.

Regarding contact arrangements

'Foster carers must be clear from the placement plan what delegated responsibility they have to make day-to-day decisions about contact arrangements.'
(Statutory guidance paragraph 3.27)

Standard 9.7   Foster carers understand what decisions about contact are delegated to them, in line with the child's care plan, and make those decisions in the child's best interests.

Regarding health

Standard 6.5   Children's health is promoted in accordance with their placement plan and foster carers are clear about what responsibilities and decisions are delegated to them and where consent for medical treatment needs to be obtained.

Regarding leisure

Standard 7.3   Foster carers understand what is in the child's placement plan and *have clarity* about decisions they can make about the day to day arrangements for the child, including such matters as education, leisure activities, overnight stays, holidays, and personal issues such as hair cuts.

Regarding education

'Foster carers should be clear, in relation to each placement, what level of decision making has been delegated to them in relation to the child's education, such as whether or not they are authorised to sign permission slips for school trips and activities.'
(Statutory guidance paragraph 3.108)

Increased delegation of decision making to foster carers

The standards and statutory guidance are consistently clear that, when considering the delegation of day-to-day decision making, empowering the foster carer should be the default position.

This can be seen as part of a concerted attempt in the standards and guidance to make the experience of living in foster care as non-stigmatising and normal as possible.

Regarding leisure

'Foster carers should be given the maximum appropriate flexibility to take decisions relating to children in their care, within the framework of the agreed placement plan and the law governing parental responsibility (PR).'
(Statutory guidance paragraph 3.10)

Standard 7.4   Foster carers are supported to make reasonable and appropriate decisions within the authority delegated to them, without having to seek consent unnecessarily.

Heightened attention to delegation is anticipated by the guidance when the placement becomes long term, reflecting the greater parental role being taken by the foster carer.

'Arrangements for delegated authority should be given particular scrutiny when children are confirmed in long term or permanent placements, and attention given to how responsibilities should be shared in order to reinforce and support the long term bonds and attachments which foster carers will be expected to build with the child.'
(Statutory guidance paragraph 3.15)

Not, of course, that this concept of greater delegation of decision making to foster carers is entirely new. The most familiar example prior to the new standards is in relation to overnight stays. Ever since the Local Authority Circular LAC(2004)4 *Guidance on the Delegation of Decisions on 'Overnight Stays' for Looked After Children*, fostering providers and local authorities have been encouraged to delegate greater levels of decision making to foster carers. This is a good example of the new standards and guidance consolidating initiatives implemented since 2002.

Standard 7.7   Children can stay overnight, holiday with friends, or friends and relatives of their foster carer, or go on schools trips, subject to requirements of the care/placement plan, if foster carers consider it appropriate in individual circumstances. CRB checks are not normally sought as a precondition.

The statutory guidance explicitly links this increased level of delegation to the theme of the foster carer as a parental figure.

> *'Parents make judgements on whether or not there are known risks to staying in a particular household or visiting relatives, and similar judgements should normally be made for children in foster care by their responsible carers.'*
> (Statutory guidance paragraph 3.17)

Proportionate approach to risk assessment

Linked to the delegation of decision making regarding overnights, foster carers are encouraged to promote a culture which accepts the existence of risk. Here we can see again the ambition to normalise foster care as far as possible.

Standard 4.4   Foster carers encourage children to take appropriate risks as a normal part of growing up.

> *'Whilst it is normal for foster carers, like parents, to want to avoid unnecessary risks, excessive caution is unhelpful. Children and young people need to be exposed to some risks, proportionate to their age and understanding. They need to be encouraged to make friends, participate in sports and outdoor activities, to be able to stay overnight with friends and explore the world they live in without excessive constraints.'*
> (Statutory guidance paragraph 3.63)

The foster placement as a family home

This repeated emphasis upon normalisation and the parental nature of the foster carer's role can be seen as part of a theme running through the guidance and standards to help the foster child feel like a member of a *family home* rather than a "placement" in a care system.

Regarding the provision of a suitable environment

Standard 10.3   Avoidable hazards are removed as is consistent with a *family home*.

Regarding preparation for a placement

Standard 11.4   Children are given free access to the household facilities as would be consistent with reasonable arrangements in a *family home*.

2 The child as an active agent of change

A heightened commitment to involving children recurs throughout the new standards and statutory guidance, symbolised most obviously by placing consultation and participation in the very first standard.

Managing and understanding risks for themselves

Children are not to be regarded, the new standards imply, as the passive recipients of services. They should be encouraged and supported to take an appropriate measure of personal responsibility for managing their own risks.

Regarding safeguarding

Standard 4.4   Children are helped to understand how to keep themselves safe, including when outside of the household or when using the internet or social media.

Regarding missing from care

Standard 5.8   Children are helped to understand the dangers and risks of leaving the foster home without permission and are made aware of where they can access help if they consider running away.

Regarding health

Standard 6.2   Children understand their health needs, how to maintain a healthy lifestyle and to make informed decisions about their own health.

Perhaps the most clear example of this self-management of risk relates to the administration of medication, although the related statutory guidance (paragraph 3.60) is keen to stress that the child must be deemed to be sufficiently responsible.

Regarding medication

Standard 6.10   Children who wish to, and who can safely keep and take their own medication, do so.

Resilience

Given this recurrent emphasis upon empowering children, it is perhaps not surprising that the concept of resilience, which found no place in the 2002 standards, becomes an important theme in the new version.

Regarding consultation and participation

Standard 2.2   Foster carers are supported to promote children's social and emotional development, and to enable children to develop emotional *resilience* and positive self-esteem.

Standard 2.6   Children develop skills and emotional *resilience* that will prepare them for independent living.

Regarding the preparation for adulthood

Standard 12.1   Children are supported to develop positive self-esteem and emotional *resilience*.

'....young people who are looked after must, as they move towards adulthood, be provided with a personal adviser (PA) who should act as a focal point for planning the transition to adulthood so that they are encouraged to develop the skills and resilience *they will need to achieve their aspirations.'*
(Statutory guidance paragraph 3.121)

Even when the term resilience is not specifically used, the concept's focus upon identifying the strengths and talents of children can be evidenced across a range of other standards.

Regarding the promotion of positive behaviour

Standard 3.1   Foster carers have high expectations of all of the foster children in their household.

Regarding health

Standard 6.3   Children are encouraged to participate in a range of positive activities that contribute to their physical and emotional health.

Regarding leisure

Standard 7.1   Children develop their emotional, intellectual, social, creative and physical skills through the accessible and stimulating environment created within the foster home. Children are supported to take part in school based and out of school activities.

Regarding education

Standard 8.4   Children are helped by their foster carer to achieve their educational or training goals and foster carers are supported to work with a child's education provider to maximise each child's achievement and to minimise any underachievement.

Managing transitions

One of the aspects of the care system most likely to undermine a child's sense of empowerment is moving in and out of foster placements with little or no warning. Surveys of the views and concerns of foster children have consistently emphasised their wish to be actively consulted about placement moves, and their distaste for moving at short notice or for systemic reasons unconnected to their welfare.

This is a theme strongly picked up in the new care planning regulations and has clear echoes throughout the new fostering standards.

Regarding preparation for placements

Standard 11.3   Unless an emergency placement makes it impossible, children are given information about the foster carer before arrival, and any information (including where appropriate, photographic information) they need or reasonably request about the placement, in a format appropriate to their age and understanding. Wherever possible, children are able to visit the foster carer's home and to talk with the foster carers in private prior to a placement decision being made. Children can bring their favourite possessions into the foster carer's home.

This is undoubtedly a very challenging standard in the current fostering climate, but its commitment to involving children actively in the preparation stages of a placement could hardly be clearer.

The new standards also require children to be actively informed of the reasons for a placement coming to end.

Regarding the ending of placements

Standard 11.5   Where children are leaving the foster family, they are helped to understand the reasons why they are leaving. Children are supported during the transition to their new placement, to independent living or to their parental home.

One of the most ambitious aspects of the new standards, guidance and regulations concerns the avoidance of an abrupt end to placements when young people reach adulthood. The statutory guidance and standards now require fostering services to have a policy position regarding how to support young people into adulthood.

Regarding the transition to adulthood

Standard 12.4   The fostering service has a policy and practical arrangements which enable children to remain with their foster carer(s) into legal adulthood, for example so that s/he may develop appropriate life skills before being required to move to more independent accommodation. Any such decisions are agreed with foster carers at a placement meeting and are detailed in a child's placement plan.

3 The importance of relationships

A growing body of social care research over the last decade supports the truism that high quality foster care is all about relationships, its success dependent upon a combination of the quality of the relationship between the child and the foster carer alongside an understanding of the relationship between the child and the birth family.

The relationship between the child and foster carer

This importance of the relationship between the foster carer and the child is repeatedly identified in the new standards and guidance as one of the principal means of achieving good outcomes. The guidance describes this theme as one of the 'values underpinning' the standards:

> *'...the central importance of the child's relationship with their foster carer will be acknowledged and the work of the wider team around the child will be undertaken in a way that strengthens and supports the role of the foster carer.'*
> (Statutory guidance paragraph 2.5)

Standard 3, for example, explicitly places behaviour management in the context of positive relationship-building.

Regarding promoting positive behaviour and relationships

Standard 3.3   Children are able to develop and practice skills to build and maintain positive relationships, be assertive and to resolve conflicts positively.

An open and trusting relationship is also seen as one of the key means of safeguarding children.

Regarding safeguarding

Standard 4.3   Foster carers make positive relationships with children, generate a culture of openness and trust and are aware of and alert to any signs or symptoms that might indicate a child is at risk of harm.

The foster carer's advocacy role

Reflecting this emphasis upon relationships, the phrase 'fostering service' in the 2002 standards is often replaced in the new standards by reference to a specific individual, such as the foster carer, the child or a particular professional role. In relation to health, for example, the repeated references to 'the fostering service' in the 2002 standards have all been replaced by descriptions of the outputs sought for the foster carer or the child.

This is more than a matter of style. There is now an added expectation that, based upon forming positive relationships, foster carers should advocate for the children in their care, in much the same way as a "good parent" would.

Regarding health

Standard 6.6   Children's wishes and feelings are sought and taken into account in their health care, according to their understanding, and foster carers *advocate* on behalf of children.

Regarding education

Standard 8.6   Foster carers maintain regular contact with each child's school and other education settings, attending all parents' meetings as appropriate and *advocating* for the child where appropriate.

Standard 8.7   Foster carers engage and work with schools, colleges and other organisations to support children's education, including *advocating* to help overcome any problems the child may be experiencing in their education setting.

This advocacy role in relation to education is very closely linked with the parental nature of the foster carer's role highlighted earlier in this chapter, described here as 'pushy' rather than good, reasonable or responsible.

> *'They [the foster carers] will require sufficient understanding of the education system to* advocate *on behalf of a child, to be the "pushy parent" where the child may be experiencing difficulties in their educational setting.'*
> (Statutory guidance paragraph 3.104)

The foster carer and contact

One notable exception to the general trend away from references to the "fostering service" towards "the foster carer" relates to contact. The 2002 standards set out an expectation that, under the auspices of the fostering service, the foster carer records the impact of contact arrangements upon the child (2002, 10.9). In the 2011 standards this expectation is expressed as follows.

Regarding contact

Standard 9.5   The fostering service feeds back to the responsible authority any significant reactions a child has to contact arrangements or visits with any person.

This is one area where the role of the foster carer seems to have diminished since the last standards were drafted, with contact increasingly taking place away the foster home and out of sight of the foster carer. Unlike the relationship between the foster carer and the child, the relationship between the foster carer and the birth parent is not given much attention in the new standards, and it is perhaps significant that the emphasis upon contact in the assessment and training of foster carers in the 2002 standards (2002, 10.5) is not present in the new ones.

Nor is there any longer any reference in the new standards to the supervision of contact by the foster carer. The notion of the foster carer working 'in conjunction with the birth parent' in the 2002 standards (2002, 13.4) is less evident in the 2011 standards, perhaps a surprising development given that the majority of foster children return home.

Having identified the key themes running through the new standards, regulations and statutory guidance, the rest of this guide examines the specific changes and their practice implications in more detail, beginning with the standards.

CHAPTER TWO
What's new? What's changed?

Part 1: The National Minimum Standards

CONSULTATION AND PARTICIPATION

2011 standards	Related 2002 standard	What's new? What's changed?
Standard 1 The child's wishes and feelings and the views of those significant to them 1.1 Children's views, wishes and feelings are acted upon, unless this is contrary to their interests or adversely affects other members of the foster care household. 1.2 Children understand how their views have been taken into account and where significant wishes or concerns are not acted upon, they are helped to understand why. 1.3 Children communicate their views on all aspects of their care and support. 1.4 The views of the child, the child's family, social worker and Independent Reviewing Officer are sought regularly on the child's care, (unless in individual cases this is not appropriate). 1.5 Children have access to independent advice and support from adults who they can contact directly and in private about problems or concerns, which is appropriate to their age and understanding. Children know their rights to advocacy, and how to access an advocate and how to contact the Children's Rights Director. 1.6 Children can take up issues in the most appropriate way with support, without fear that this will result in any adverse consequences. Children receive prompt feedback on any concerns or complaints raised and are kept informed of progress. 1.7 The wishes, feelings and views of children and those significant to them are taken into account in monitoring foster carers and developing the fostering service.	11.1 The fostering service ensures that children's opinions, and those of their families and others significant to the child, are sought over all issues which are likely to affect their daily life and their future. 11.2 The fostering service ensures that all foster carers understand the importance of listening to the views of the children in their care, and are trained and supported in listening and responding to children's views. 11.3 The fostering service ensures that the opinions and views of children on all matters affecting them, including day-to-day matters, are ascertained on a regular and frequent basis and not taken for granted. 11.4 Suitable means are provided, frequently, for any child with communication difficulties to make their wishes and feelings known regarding their care and treatment. 11.5 The fostering service ensures that children in foster care know how to raise any concerns or complaints, and ensures that they receive prompt feedback on any concerns or complaints raised.	*Throughout the 2011 standards, a heightened priority is given to listening to and involving children, symbolised by placing participation and consultation in the opening standard.* ● New expectation that feedback is provided to children when their significant wishes are not acted upon, not just in relation to their complaints or concerns (1.2). ● The duty to consult with the child's family and those 'significant to the child' in the 2002 standards is specified further in the 2011 standards to include the IRO and the child's social worker (1.4). ● Children's rights, independent support and advocacy are specifically mentioned in the 2011 standards, as well as how to contact the Children's Rights Director (1.5). ● The link between consultation with children and monitoring the quality of the foster care provision is stronger in the 2011 standards (1.7). ● The reference to children with communication difficulties in the 2002 standards is not present in the 2011 version. Instead, communication needs are addressed in 16.5 in relation to the children's guide and in 25.12 in relation to effective management and monitoring.

IDENTITY AND DIVERSITY

2011 standards	Related 2002 standard	What's new? What's changed?
Standard 2 Promoting a positive identity, potential and valuing diversity through individualised care **2.1** Children are provided with personalised care that meets their needs and promotes all aspects of their individual identity. **2.2** Foster carers are supported to promote children's social and emotional development, and to enable children to develop emotional resilience and positive self-esteem. **2.3** Foster carers meet children's individual needs as set out in the child's placement plan as part of the wider family context. **2.4** Children exercise choice in the food that they eat, and are able to prepare their own meals and snacks, within the context of the foster family's decision making and the limits that a responsible parent would set. **2.5** Children exercise choice and independence in the clothes and personal requisites that they buy and have these needs met, within the context of the foster family's decision making and the reasonable limits that a responsible parent would set. **This sub-standard is not applicable to short break placements.** **2.6** Children develop skills and emotional resilience that will prepare them for independent living. **2.7** Children receive a personal allowance appropriate to their age and understanding, that is consistent with their placement plan. **This sub-standard is not applicable to short break placements.**	**7.1** The fostering service ensures that children and young people, and their families, are provided with foster care services which value diversity and promote equality. **7.2** Each child and her/his family have access to foster care services which recognise and address her/his needs in terms of gender, religion, ethnic origin, language, culture, disability and sexuality. If a foster placement has to be made in an emergency and no suitable placement is available in terms of the above, then steps are taken to achieve the above within 6 weeks. **7.3** The fostering service ensures that foster carers and social workers work cooperatively to enhance the child's confidence and feeling of self-worth. Foster carers' and social workers' training covers this issue. **7.4** The fostering service ensures that their foster carers provide care which respects and preserves each child's ethnic, religious, cultural and linguistic background. Foster carers' preparation and training cover this. **7.5** The fostering service ensures that their foster carers support and encourage each child to develop skills to help her/him to deal with all forms of discrimination. Foster carers' preparation and training cover this. **7.6** Each child with a disability receives specific services and support to help her/him to maximise her/his potential and to lead as full a life as possible, including appropriate equipment and, where necessary and appropriate, adaptation of the carer's home and/or vehicle.	*The greater emphasis upon participation in standard 1 is combined in this standard with normalising the experience of being fostered. Linked to developing their resilience, children are encouraged to exercise personal choice within reasonable limits established by the responsible parenting of the foster carer. Implicit in this standard are greater and clearer levels of delegation of day-to-day decision making to the foster carer.* ● New reference to the Placement Plan (2.3 and 2.7) as a means of ensuring children's needs are met. ● New emphasis upon children's choices in relation to food and personal requisites, along with opportunities to prepare their own food, placed within 'reasonable limits' (2.5) that a 'responsible parent'(2.4 and 2.5) would set. ● The references to self-worth and confidence in the 2002 standards (2002, 7.3) are translated into the concept of resilience in the 2011 standards (2.2 and 2.6). ● References to equality and discrimination in the 2002 standards (2002, 7.5) are not present in this 2011 equivalent standard. There *is* reference to discrimination in relation to bullying in 3.6. ● There is no specific reference to a child's cultural, religious or linguistic background in the 2011 standards themselves.

2011 standards	Related 2002 standard	What's new? What's changed?
	7.7 The fostering service ensures that their foster carers give each child encouragement and equal access to opportunities to develop and pursue her/his talents, interests and hobbies. This is set out in the information provided to foster carers. Disabled children are provided with services and supports which enable them to access as wide a range of activities as is possible for them.	• Components of a child's identity in the 2002 standards (2002, 7.2) are not present in the 2011 standards, which refer more broadly to 'individual identity' (2.1). • The 2002 standards' 6 week yardstick for moving children placed in a placement that was not 'suitable' in terms of a child's identity (2002, 7.2) has gone. • Unlike the 2002 equivalent standards, there is no specific reference to disabled children in this context, except by implication in the exemptions related to short break services in 2.5 and 2.7.

PROMOTING POSITIVE BEHAVIOUR

2011 standards	Related 2002 standard	What's new? What's changed?
Standard 3 Promoting positive behaviour and relationships	9.2 Training for foster carers includes training in caring for a child who has been abused, safe caring skills, managing behaviour and recognising signs of abuse and on ways of boosting and maintaining the child's self-esteem.	*In this standard fostering is linked to good parenting, supported by an expectation of training for foster carers on behaviour management, additional support when coping with particularly challenging behaviour and full information about the child. Behaviour management is placed in the context of developing positive relationships.*
3.1 Foster carers have high expectations of all of the foster children in their household.		
3.2 Foster carers provide an environment and culture that promotes, models and supports positive behaviour.	9.4 The fostering service makes clear to the foster carers that corporal punishment is not acceptable and that this includes smacking, slapping, shaking and all other humiliating forms of treatment or punishment. This is set out clearly in written information for foster carers.	• The term 'managing behaviour' is reframed as promoting 'positive behaviour' (3.2) or 'positive care and control' (3.8).
3.3 Children are able to develop and practice skills to build and maintain positive relationships, be assertive and to resolve conflicts positively.		• New emphasis upon encouraging children to take responsibility for their own behaviour (3.4).
3.4 Children are encouraged to take responsibility for their behaviour in a way that is appropriate to their age and abilities.	9.6 The fostering service ensures that foster carers are aware of the particular vulnerability of looked after children and their susceptibility to bullying and procedures are in place to recognise, record and address any instance of bullying and to help foster carers cope with it.	• New stronger link between bullying and discrimination (3.6).
3.5 Foster carers respect the child's privacy and confidentiality, in a manner that is consistent with good parenting.		• New emphasis upon offering advice and support to foster carers when caring for children with 'very challenging behaviour' (3.7).
3.6 Foster carers have positive strategies for effectively supporting children where they encounter discrimination or bullying wherever this occurs.	9.7 Each foster carer is provided with full information about the foster child and her/his family to enable the carer to protect the foster child, their own children, other children for whom they have responsibility and themselves.	• New policy and training expectations in this area, extending beyond the prohibition of specific sanctions (2002, 9.4) to include the de-escalation of conflicts and disputes (3.8).
3.7 Foster carers receive support on how to manage their responses and feelings arising from caring for children, particularly where children display very challenging behaviour, and understand how children's previous experiences can manifest in challenging behaviour.	24.6 The fostering service gives the foster carer access to all relevant information to help the child understand and come to terms with past events. (Where necessary information is not forthcoming from the responsible authority, a copy of the written request for information is kept.)	• New expectation that the fostering service's written policy is made available to the placing authority, the child and the child's parents/carers (3.8) prior to placement except in emergencies.

2011 standards	Related 2002 standard	What's new? What's changed?
3.8 All foster carers receive training in positive care and control of children, including training in de-escalating problems and disputes. The fostering service has a clear written policy on managing behaviour, which includes supporting positive behaviour, de-escalation of conflicts and discipline. The fostering service's policy is made clear to the responsible authority/placing authority, child and parent/s or carers before the placement begins or, in an emergency placement, at the time of the placement.		• New context for gaining up-to-date information from the responsible local authority (3.9). Although similar to the 2002 standard (2002, 24.6) regarding records, the link with behaviour management is new.
3.9 Each foster carer is aware of all the necessary information available to the fostering service about a child's circumstances, including any significant recent events, to help the foster carer understand and predict the child's needs and behaviours and support the child within their household. The fostering service follows up with the responsible authority where all such necessary information has not been provided by the authority.		• The expectation to convey 'necessary' information about the child to the foster carer (3.9) is now related to predicting and responding to needs and behaviour rather than child protection (2002, 9.7).
3.10 The fostering service's approach to care minimises the need for police involvement to deal with challenging behaviour and avoids criminalising children unnecessarily.		• New emphasis upon avoiding the criminalisation of foster children (3.10).

SAFEGUARDING

2011 standards	Related 2002 standard	What's new? What's changed?
Standard 4 Safeguarding children 4.1 Children's safety and welfare is promoted in all fostering placements. Children are protected from abuse and other forms of significant harm (e.g. sexual or labour exploitation). 4.2 Foster carers actively safeguard and promote the welfare of foster children. 4.3 Foster carers make positive relationships with children, generate a culture of openness and trust and are aware of and alert to any signs or symptoms that might indicate a child is at risk of harm. 4.4 Foster carers encourage children to take appropriate risks as a normal part of growing up. Children are helped to understand how to keep themselves safe, including when outside of the household or when using the internet or social media. 4.5 The service implements a proportionate approach to any risk assessment. 4.6 Foster carers are trained in appropriate safe care practice, including skills to care for children who have been abused. For foster carers who offer placements to disabled children, this includes training specifically on issues affecting disabled children. 4.7 The fostering service works effectively in partnership with other agencies concerned with child protection, e.g. the responsible authority, schools, hospitals, general practitioners, etc., and does not work in isolation from them.	9.1 The fostering service protects each child or young person from all forms of abuse, neglect, exploitation and deprivation. 9.2 Training for foster carers includes training in caring for a child who has been abused, safe caring skills, managing behaviour and recognising signs of abuse and on ways of boosting and maintaining the child's self-esteem. 9.3 Safe caring guidelines are provided, based on a written policy, for each foster home, in consultation with the carer and everyone else in the household. The guidelines are cleared with the child's social worker and are explained clearly and appropriately to the child.	*The importance of the relationship between the foster carer and the child in standard 3 is also found in this standard. Children are not seen as passive in relation to safeguarding, and again there is reference to normalising the experience of fostering, with children encouraged to take appropriate risks. The fostering service is expected to work collaboratively with other agencies.* ● New reference to sexual and labour exploitation (4.1). ● New emphasis upon the relationship between foster carers and children as a means of safeguarding them (4.3). ● New emphasis upon 'appropriate' risk taking (4.4) and a 'proportionate' approach to risk assessment (4.5). ● New reference to the internet and social media (4.4). ● New emphasis upon disability-specific safer caring training for those caring for disabled children (4.6). ● New emphasis upon partnership working for fostering services in relation to safeguarding (4.7). ● The expectation in the 2002 standards (2002, 9.3) that household-specific safe caring guidelines are cleared with the child's social worker has gone.

MISSING FROM CARE

2011 standards	Related 2002 standard	What's new? What's changed?

Standard 5 Missing from care

5.1 The care and support provided to children minimises the risk that they will go missing and reduces the risk of harm should the child go missing.

5.2 Foster carers know and implement what the fostering service and the responsible authority's policy is in relation to children going missing.

5.3 Foster carers are aware of, and do not exceed, the measures they can take to prevent a child leaving without permission under current legislation and Government guidance.

5.4 Children who are absent from the foster home without consent, but whose whereabouts are known or thought to be known by carers or staff, are protected in line with the fostering service's written procedure.

5.5 The fostering service and foster carers take appropriate action to find children who are missing, including working alongside the police where appropriate.

5.6 If a child is absent from the fostering home and their whereabouts are not known (i.e. the child is missing), the fostering service's procedures are compatible with the local Runaway and Missing from Home and Care (RMFHC) protocols and procedures applicable to the area where each foster home is located.

5.7 Where children placed out of authority go missing, the manager of the fostering service follows the local RMFHC protocol. They also comply with, and make foster carers aware of, any other processes required by the responsible authority, specified in the individual child's care plan and in the RMFHC protocol covering the authority responsible for the child's care.

9.8 The fostering service makes sure that the foster carer has a clear written procedure for use if the foster child is missing from home.

Although nearly all of this material is new in terms of the standards, reflecting the substantial statutory guidance[1] on this topic issued since 2002, much of it may be familiar to fostering services through local protocols.

- There are new policy expectations in relation to ensuring foster carers know the steps they can take to prevent a child leaving (5.3), how to respond to a child's unauthorised absence (5.4), how to respond when a child is missing (5.5, 5.6), and an awareness of the local *and* responsible authority's relevant protocols (5.6 and 5.7).

- New expectation to advise children of the risks of running away and where they can access help (5.8), similar to the emphasis upon children taking some responsibility for their own safety in standard 4.

- New expectation to convene a meeting to explore the reasons behind a child going missing and prevent recurrence (5.9).

- New recording demands made of fostering services, including potential sharing of information with the child's parents (5.10).

---

1 Statutory Guidance, *Children who Run Away and Go Missing from Home and Care* (DCSF, 2009)

2011 standards	Related 2002 standard	What's new? What's changed?
5.8 Children are helped to understand the dangers and risks of leaving the foster home without permission and are made aware of where they can access help if they consider running away.		
5.9 Where a child goes missing and there is concern for their welfare, or at the request of a child who has been missing, the fostering service arranges a meeting in private between the child and the responsible authority to consider the reasons for their going missing. The fostering service considers with the responsible authority and foster carer what action should be taken to prevent the child going missing in future. Any concerns arising about the foster carer or the placement are addressed, as far as is possible, in conjunction with the responsible authority.		
5.10 Written records kept by the fostering service where a child goes missing detail action taken by foster carers, the circumstances of the child's return, any reasons given by the child for running away from the foster home and any action taken in the light of those reasons. This information is shared with the responsible authority and, where appropriate, the child's parents.		

HEALTH

2011 standards	Related 2002 standard	What's new? What's changed?
Standard 6 Promoting good health and wellbeing	12.1 The fostering service ensures that it provides foster care services which help each child or young person in foster care to receive health care which meets her/his needs for physical, emotional and social development, together with information and training appropriate to her/his age and understanding to enable informed participation in decisions about her/his health needs.	***Children are encouraged to take responsibility for their own health in this standard, supported by foster carers who understand which decisions lie within their discretion and who are encouraged to advocate on their behalf.***
6.1 Children's physical and emotional and social development needs are promoted.		
6.2 Children understand their health needs, how to maintain a healthy lifestyle and to make informed decisions about their own health.		• Heightened emphasis upon 'healthy lifestyle' (6.2) and 'positive activities' (6.3) for foster children, building upon the 'health promotion' cited in the 2002 standards (2002, 12.5 and 12.6).
6.3 Children are encouraged to participate in a range of positive activities that contribute to their physical and emotional health.	12.2 The fostering service is informed about health services, including specialist services, available in the area it covers and takes this into account when finding/suggesting a foster carer for a child. The fostering service ensures that no placement is made which prevents a child from continuing to receive the specialist health care services they need.	• The need for *prompt* access to a range of health services, including specialist services, is new (6.4).
6.4 Children have prompt access to doctors and other health professionals, including specialist services (in conjunction with the responsible authority), when they need these services.		• New focus upon the need for clarity in relation to the delegation of responsibilities and health-related decisions, including consent for medical treatement, to foster carers (6.5).
6.5 Children's health is promoted in accordance with their placement plan and foster carers are clear about what responsibilities and decisions are delegated to them and where consent for medical treatment needs to be obtained.	12.3 Before a placement begins, the carer is provided with as full a description as possible of the health needs of a child and clear procedures governing consent for the child to receive medical treatment. Where there is an agency placement, the responsible authority provides this information to the agency and the agency passes it on to the carer. If full details of the health needs are not available before placement, a high priority is given to ensuring that the information is obtained and passed to the foster carer once the placement is made.	• New training and guidance expectations for foster carers in relation to complex health needs (6.8) and the management and administration of medication (6.10).
6.6 Children's wishes and feelings are sought and taken into account in their health care, according to their understanding, and foster carers advocate on behalf of children.		• New, more explicit expectations regarding medication, including secure storage by the foster carer (6.9), although in practice this expectation has generally already been accepted with reference to 'avoidable hazards' in the 2002 standards (2002, 6.6).
6.7 Foster carers receive sufficient training on health and hygiene issues and first aid, with particular emphasis on health promotion and communicable diseases.		
6.8 Foster carers receive guidance and training to provide appropriate care if looking after children with complex health needs.	12.4 The carer is provided with a written health record for each child placed in their care; this is updated during the placement and moves with the child. Depending upon age and understanding, the child has access to and understands the health record kept by the fostering service.	
6.9 Medicines kept in the foster home are stored safely and are accessible only by those for whom they are intended.		

2011 standards	Related 2002 standard	What's new? What's changed?
6.10 Foster carers are trained in the management and administration of medication. Prescribed medication is only given to the child for whom it was prescribed, and in accordance with the prescription. Children who wish to, and who can safely keep and take their own medication, do so.	**12.5** Each carer is given basic training on health and hygiene issues and first aid, with particular emphasis on health promotion and communicable diseases.	• The 2002 standards seek 'informed participation' by young people (2002, 12.1) whereas in the 2011 standards children are seen as more active in relation to their own health care, with expectations that they understand their own health needs (6.2), that their wishes and feelings in relation to health care are *sought* (6.6) and that they may 'keep and take their own medication' (6.10).
6.11 Foster carers keep a written record of all medication, treatment and first aid given to children during their placement.	**12.6** The fostering service makes clear to the carer their role in terms of helping to promote the health of any child in their care. This includes:	
6.12 Any physical adaptations or equipment needed for the appropriate care of the children are provided to foster carers.	• registering a child with a doctor or dentist when necessary • taking the child to any health appointments, including dental and optician appointments, when required; • helping her/him to access the services that she/he needs • giving attention to health issues in everyday care of the child, including diet, personal hygiene, health promotion issues, etc; • acting as an advocate on the child's behalf.	• New recording expectations regarding *all* medication given to children by foster carers (6.11) rather than the broader 'supplying information' in the 2002 standards (2002, 12.8). In practice, the expectation of the 2002 standards to maintain a health record (2002, 12.4) resulted in a demand for a running record of medication.
	12.7 The fostering service has good links with health agencies and help the carer to secure services for the child when necessary.	• The references to physical adaptations and equipment are now placed here in the context of health (6.12) rather than 'Valuing Diversity' in the 2002 standards (2002, 7.6)
	12.8 The fostering service requires foster carers to supply information about the child's health needs for the planning and review process.	

LEISURE

2011 standards	Related 2002 standard	What's new? What's changed?
Standard 7 Leisure activities 7.1 Children develop their emotional, intellectual, social, creative and physical skills through the accessible and stimulating environment created within the foster home. Children are supported to take part in school based and out of school activities. 7.2 Children pursue individual interests and hobbies. They take part in a range of activities, including leisure activities and trips. 7.3 Foster carers understand what is in the child's placement plan and have clarity about decisions they can make about the day to day arrangements for the child, including such matters as education, leisure activities, overnight stays, holidays, and personal issues such as hair cuts. 7.4 Foster carers are supported to make reasonable and appropriate decisions within the authority delegated to them, without having to seek consent unnecessarily. 7.5 Children have permission to take part in age appropriate peer activities as would normally be granted by a reasonable parent to their children, within the framework of the placement plan. Decision-making and any assessment of risk to the child should be undertaken on the same basis as a reasonable parent would do. 7.6 Children are encouraged and enabled to make and sustain friendships, which may involve reciprocal arrangements to visit friends' homes. 7.7 Children can stay overnight, holiday with friends, or friends and relatives of their foster carer, or go on school trips, subject to requirements of the care/placement plan, if foster carers consider it appropriate in individual circumstances. CRB checks are not normally sought as a precondition.	7.7 The fostering service ensures that their foster carers give each child encouragement and equal access to opportunities **to develop and pursue her/his talents, interests and hobbies.** This is set out in the information provided to foster carers. Disabled children are provided with services and supports which enable them to access as wide a range of activities as is possible for them.	***The development of the foster child's resilience underpins this standard, with children being encouraged to develop interests and maintain friendships. The recurring theme in the standards regarding the delegation of day-to-day decision making to foster carers is particularly strong here, with two references to discretion regarding overnight stays.*** • This 2011 standard is a considerable expansion upon the brief reference to talents, interests and hobbies in the 2002 standards (2002, 7.7). • New emphasis upon the need for *clarity* regarding the extent of the delegated authority to foster carers regarding 'day-to-day arrangements' (7.3). • New emphasis upon *greater* delegation to foster carers, with the notion of 'reasonable' decisions and acting as a 'reasonable parent' in 7.4 and 7.5 echoing the 'the responsible parent' concept of standards 2.4 and 2.5. • Although the 2002 standards made reference to friendship in relation to contact, standard 7.6 is an example of a new emphasis upon friendship (7.6). • Although based upon LAC (2004)4, standards 7.3 and 7.7 are new references to the delegation of decisions about overnight stays in the standards.

EDUCATION

2011 standards	Related 2002 standard	What's new? What's changed?
Standard 8 Promoting educational attainment **8.1** Children, including pre-school children and older children, have a foster home which promotes a learning environment and supports their development. **8.2** Children have access to a range of educational resources to support their learning and have opportunities beyond the school day to engage in activities which promote learning. **8.3** Children are supported to attend school, or alternative provision, regularly. **8.4** Children are helped by their foster carer to achieve their educational or training goals and foster carers are supported to work with a child's education provider to maximise each child's achievement and to minimise any underachievement. **8.5** The fostering service has, and is fully implementing, a written education policy that promotes and values children's education and is understood by foster carers. **8.6** Foster carers maintain regular contact with each child's school and other education settings, attending all parents' meetings as appropriate and advocating for the child where appropriate. **8.7** Foster carers engage and work with schools, colleges and other organisations to support children's education, including advocating to help overcome any problems the child may be experiencing in their education setting. Foster carers have up-to-date information about each child's educational progress and school attendance record.	**13.1** The fostering service gives a high priority to meeting the educational needs of each child or young person in foster care and ensures that she/he is encouraged to attain her/his full potential. **13.2** The fostering service gives high priority to helping their foster carers to meet a child's education needs. **13.3** The fostering service requires foster carers to contribute to the assessment of the child's educational needs and progress for the planning and review process. The fostering service helps the foster carer to contribute to the delivery of any personal education plan. **13.4** The foster carer's role in school contact, e.g. parents evenings, open days, discussions with teachers, in conjunction with the birth parent where appropriate and in line with the care plan, is clearly laid out in the placement agreement. **13.5** The fostering service ensures that their foster carers provide an environment in which education and learning are valued; and that the foster carer establishes an expectation of regular attendance at school, and supports the child's full participation through provision of necessary uniform and equipment, support for completion of homework, and financial and other support for attending school trips and after school activities. **13.6** The fostering service has information systems to demonstrate the educational attainment of the children and young people in their foster care services and to demonstrate the numbers excluded from school.	*The definition of education is extended in this standard beyond schooling to include the provision of a learning environment, with a greater emphasis upon the role of the foster carer. The implication of the standard is that the foster carer should advocate and participate in the child's education just as a parent should, although the 'responsible parent' phrase is not used here.* ● New mention of education in relation to pre-school children (8.1). ● The reference in the 2002 standards to after school activities and trips 2002, 13.5) is extended to 'opportunities beyond the school day', implying that these may not be linked directly with schooling (8.2). ● New emphasis upon foster carers taking on supportive and advocacy roles in relation to education (8.4, 8.6 and 8.7). ● New expectation to have an education policy which is understood by foster carers (8.5). ● The monitoring expectations in the 2002 standards regarding attainment and exclusions 2002, 13.6) have changed into requirements to *provide* this information to foster carers (8.7). ● The reference to the PEP 2002, 13.3) has gone. ● The reference to working 'in conjunction with birth parents where appropriate' in the 2002 standards (2002, 13.4) has gone.

2011 standards	Related 2002 standard	What's new? What's changed?
	13.7 The fostering service makes clear its expectations (in relation to school-day responsibilities) of foster carers and the arrangements which will be put in place if any child in their care is not in school. Those arrangements include structured occupation during school hours.	
	13.8 The foster placement agreement identifies where financial responsibility lies for all school costs, including school uniform, school trips and school equipment.	

CONTACT

2011 standards	Related 2002 standard	What's new? What's changed?
Standard 9 Promoting and supporting contact 9.1 Children are supported and encouraged to maintain and develop family contacts and friendships, subject to any limitations or provisions set out in their care plan, placement plan and any court order. 9.2 Foster carers are given practical help to support appropriate contact, including financial help where needed, alongside support to manage any difficult emotional or other issues that the child and foster carer may have as a result of contact. 9.3 Emergency restrictions on contact are only made to protect the child from significant risk to their safety or welfare and are communicated to the responsible authority within 24 hours of being imposed. 9.4 Ongoing restriction on communication by the child is agreed by the child's responsible authority, takes the child's wishes and feelings into account and is regularly reviewed in collaboration with the responsible authority. 9.5 The fostering service feeds back to the responsible authority any significant reactions a child has to contact arrangements or visits with any person. 9.6 When deciding whether to offer a placement, the fostering service works with the responsible authority in giving consideration to how the child's contact with family and significant others will be supported, particularly where a child is placed at a distance from home.	10.1 The fostering service makes sure that each child or young person in foster care is encouraged to maintain and develop family contacts and friendships as set out in her/his care plan and/or foster placement agreement. 10.2 There are clear procedures setting out how appropriate contact arrangements for each child in foster care are to be established, maintained, monitored and reviewed. 10.3 The fostering service considers the need for and benefits of appropriate contact for the child when finding/suggesting a suitable foster carer. Attention is paid to supporting contact where the child is placed outside of the area. 10.4 The views of the child or young person are sought and given weight in determining contact arrangements. 10.5 In assessment and training of carers, the fostering service stresses the importance of foster carers helping a child to maintain appropriate contacts and covers the skills required to encourage and facilitate such contacts. 10.6 Except where an overriding requirement exists, e.g. a court order, the fostering service ensures that contact does not take place until the child's social worker has carried out a risk assessment and arrangements made for any supervision that is needed.	*In an attempt to address the well-evidenced tendency for contact to diminish the longer a child is in care, this standard establishes additional and urgent scrutiny whenever contact is unexpectedly reduced. As in other standards, greater clarity is demanded regarding the delegation of decision making to the foster carer, though the foster carer's direct role in supervising and recording the impact of contact on the child seems lessened.* ● An acknowledgement of the impact of contact upon the *foster carer* as well as the child is evidenced in 9.2. ● New expectations to notify the responsible authority of any emergency restrictions on contact within 24 hours (9.3) and to agree any ongoing restrictions (9.4). ● Whereas the 2002 standards outlined expectations that children are consulted in relation to contact arrangements in general (2002, 10.4), in the new standards consultation is only mentioned in relation to any *restrictions* (9.4). ● In the 2002 standards, the *foster carer* is specified to record the child's reaction to contact (2002, 10.9); in the 2011 standards this becomes an expectation of the fostering *service* (9.5). ● The assessment and training requirements for foster carers regarding contact in the 2002 standards (2002, 10.5) have gone.

2011 standards	Related 2002 standard	What's new? What's changed?
9.7 Foster carers understand what decisions about contact are delegated to them, in line with the child's care plan, and make those decisions in the child's best interests. **The above standards are not required for short breaks. For children in short breaks the foster carer must know how to contact parents and maintain such contact as has been agreed in the short break care plan.**	**10.7** The fostering service provides help and support to the carer in dealing with any difficult contact issues that may arise. The fostering service provider ensures that the role of the foster carer in supporting contact arrangements, including any arrangements for the supervision of contact, are clearly articulated in the Foster Placement Agreement. **10.8** Financial support is provided to the carer for transport or other costs involved in ensuring contacts take place at the desired frequency and in the most suitable place. **10.9** The fostering service ensures that the carer records outcomes of contact arrangements and their perceived impact on the child; this information is fed back to the child's social worker.	• The emphasis upon clarity of the foster carer's *role* in relation to contact in the 2002 standards (2002, 10.7) has altered to become clarity regarding which *decisions* regarding contact lie within the discretion of the foster carer (9.7). • The reference in the 2002 standards in relation to foster carers supervising contact (2002, 10.7) has gone. • The 2002 requirement for a social worker risk assessment prior to any contact arrangements (2002, 10.6) has gone. • The regulatory exemption regarding contact (see regulation 42) is modified here by reference to the short break care plan, drawn from the Care Planning Regulations 2010.

PHYSICAL ENVIRONMENT

2011 standards	Related 2002 standard	What's new? What's changed?
Standard 10 Providing a suitable physical environment for the foster child **10.1** The foster home can comfortably accommodate all who live there including where appropriate any suitable aids and adaptations provided and fitted by suitably trained staff when caring for a disabled child. **10.2** The foster home is warm, adequately furnished and decorated, is maintained to a good standard of cleanliness and hygiene and is in good order throughout. Outdoor spaces which are part of the premises are safe, secure and well maintained. **10.3** Foster carers are trained in health and safety issues and have guidelines on their health and safety responsibilities. Avoidable hazards are removed as is consistent with a family home. **10.4** Foster carers understand the service's policy concerning safety for children in the foster home and in vehicles used to transport foster children. The service's policy is regularly reviewed in line with the most recent guidance from relevant bodies. **10.5** The foster home is inspected annually, without appointment, by the fostering service to make sure that it continues to meet the needs of foster children.	**6.1** The fostering service makes available foster carers who provide a safe, healthy and nurturing environment. **6.2** The foster home can comfortably accommodate all who live there. It is inspected annually to make sure that it meets the needs of foster children. **6.3** The home is warm, adequately furnished and decorated and is maintained to a good standard of cleanliness and hygiene. **6.4** Each child placed has her/his own bed and accommodation arrangements reflect the child's assessed need for privacy and space or for any specific need resulting from a disability. **6.5** If the child has been abused or has abused another child, then the child's needs and the needs of all other children in the home are assessed before any decision is made to allow sharing of bedrooms. The outcome of that assessment is recorded in writing. **6.6** The home and immediate environment are free of avoidable hazards that might expose a child to risk of injury or harm and contain safety barriers and equipment appropriate to the child's age, development and level of ability. **6.7** The foster carer's preparation and training cover health and safety issues and the carer is provided with written guidelines on their health and safety responsibilities. **6.8** Where the foster carer is expected to provide transport for the child, the fostering service ensures this is safe and appropriate to the child's needs.	*Much of this 2011 standard is similar in content, though re-ordered, to the 2002 version. There is greater specification regarding room sharing along with an emphasis upon the homeliness of the environment.* ● New reference to the 'family home,' part of a broader agenda to ensure that living in foster care feels more like being a part of a family rather than part of a care system (10.3). ● New expectation to review the health and safety policy 'regularly' (10.4). ● The annual unannounced visit set out in the 2002 standards (2002, 22.6) is repeated in two 2011 standards: 10.5, which outlines the need to visit 'without appointment' annually in the context of a standard about the foster carer's home environment; and 21.8 (see below) in the context of the social worker's supervision of the foster carer. ● New expectation that, unless there is a specific agreement in place, any foster child over three has their own bedroom (10.6). ● The elements within the assessment required prior to room sharing in the 2002 standards (2002, 6.5) are now extended in the 2011 standards beyond the consideration of any history of abuse to include bullying, the wishes and feelings of the children and 'all other pertinent facts' (10.6). ● Although the reference to visits by the inspectorate to foster carers in the 2002 standards has gone (2002, 6.9) the requirement to comply with a visit by Ofsted is set out in Schedule 5 of the 2011 regulations.

2011 standards	Related 2002 standard	What's new? What's changed?
10.6 In the foster home, each child over the age of three should have their own bedroom. If this is not possible, the sharing of a bedroom is agreed by each child's responsible authority and each child has their own area within the bedroom. Before seeking agreement for the sharing of a bedroom, the fostering service provider takes into account any potential for bullying, any history of abuse or abusive behaviour, the wishes of the children concerned and all other pertinent facts. The decision making process and outcome of the assessment are recorded in writing where bedroom sharing is agreed.	6.9 Foster carers understand that they may be interviewed or visited as part of the Commission's inspection process. 18.5 There is a comprehensive health and safety policy for carers, children and staff which covers all legal requirements.	

PREPARING FOR A PLACEMENT

2011 standards	Related 2002 standard	What's new? What's changed?
Standard 11 Preparation for a placement **11.1** The service has and implements clear procedures for introducing children into the foster care placement, to the foster carer and others living in the household, which cover planned and, where permitted, emergency/immediate foster care placements. They help children understand what to expect from living in the foster home. **11.2** Children are carefully matched to a foster placement. Foster carers have full information about the child (as set out in standard 3.9). **11.3** Unless an emergency placement makes it impossible, children are given information about the foster carer before arrival, and any information (including, where appropriate, photographic information) they need or reasonably request about the placement, in a format appropriate to their age and understanding. Wherever possible, children are able to visit the foster carer's home and to talk with the foster carers in private prior to a placement decision being made. Children can bring their favourite possessions into the foster carer's home. **11.4** Children are given free access to the household facilities as would be consistent with reasonable arrangements in a family home. Foster carers explain everyday household rules and expectations to children.	**8.7** Where practicable, each child has the opportunity for a period of introduction to a proposed foster carer so she/he can express an informed view about the placement and become familiar with the carer, the carer's family, any other children in placement, and the home, neighbourhood and any family pets, before moving in. Information for carers explains that this approach is used when possible.	*This standard reflects the concern that children often describe feeling passive and ill-informed when moving from placement to placement in the care system, with changes being made too abruptly. The standard seeks to emphasise good quality and detailed information for the child prior to placement, and open communication once there.* ● New policy expectations in relation to planned and emergency placements (11.1). ● New expectation to provide 'full' information to the foster carer about the foster child (11.2) and to the foster child about the foster carer (11.3), including 'household rules' (11.4). ● The notion of 'reasonable arrangements' has echoes of the 'reasonable parent' in standard 7.5, alongside a repeat of the phrase 'family home' (11.4) first found in standard 10.3. ● New expectation that foster children will be able to talk to the foster carer in private prior to placement and bring favourite possessions (11.3). ● New expectation to explain the reasons for a placement coming to an end to the child (11.5). ● New emphasis upon smoothing the transition between placements (11.5) and supporting carers to maintain links post-placement (11.6).

2011 standards	Related 2002 standard	What's new? What's changed?
11.5 Where children are leaving the foster family, they are helped to understand the reasons why they are leaving. Children are supported during the transition to their new placement, to independent living or to their parental home. 11.6 Foster carers are supported to maintain links with children moving on, consistent with their care plan.		• Although the 2002 expectation that children can be enabled to express an 'informed view' of the proposed placement (2002, 8.7) has gone, the expectations outlined in 11.3 are anticipated prior to any placement decision, presumably based upon gaining the views of the child.

PROMOTING INDEPENDENCE

2011 standards	Related 2002 standard	What's new? What's changed?
Standard 12 Promoting independence and moves to adulthood and leaving care 12.1 Children are supported to: a establish positive and appropriate social and sexual relationships; b develop positive self-esteem and emotional resilience; c prepare for the world of work and/or further or higher education; d prepare for moving into their own accommodation; e develop practical skills, including shopping, buying, cooking and keeping food, washing clothes, personal self-care, and understanding and taking responsibility for personal healthcare; f develop financial capability, knowledge and skills; g know about entitlements to financial and other support after leaving care, including benefits and support from social care services. 12.2 Foster carers contribute to the development of each child's care plan, in collaboration with the child, including the pathway plan for an "eligible" child, and work collaboratively with the young person's social worker or personal adviser in implementing the plan.	14.1 The fostering service ensures that their foster care services help to develop skills, competence and knowledge necessary for adult living. 14.2 There are clear written requirements of what is expected of foster carers in terms of preparing children and young people for independent or semi-independent living. 14.3 Foster carers receive training and support to enable them to provide effective support and guidance to a young person preparing to move into independent or semi-independent living. 14.4 The fostering service ensures that foster carers understand that they need to provide all children in their care with age and developmentally appropriate opportunities for learning independence skills. 14.5 The fostering service ensures that each young person preparing to move to independent or semi-independent living is consulted about her/his future and encouraged to be actively involved in decision making processes and implementation of the Pathway Plan.	*This standard emphasises the practical skills foster children need to acquire if they are to make a successful transition to adulthood. The active role foster carers should take in relation to preparing the foster child is also evident here.* ● New, far more detailed specification about the skills and knowledge children are supported to acquire in readiness for independence (12.1). ● Echoing 2.2 and 2.6, new reference to developing resilience (12.1b). ● Greater expectations placed upon the foster carer to contribute to the Pathway Plan and to work collaboratively with the child, the child's social worker and the personal adviser (12.2). ● New reference to transitions and disabled children (12.3). ● New policy expectations enabling children to remain in foster care until adulthood (12.4). See statutory guidance paragraph 3.125 for a fuller outline of these expectations. See also standard 28.4 below regarding financial arrangements. ● New exemption from this standard for short breaks provision.

2011 standards	Related 2002 standard	What's new? What's changed?

12.3 The fostering service ensures there are comprehensive arrangements for preparing and supporting young people to make the transition to independence. This includes appropriate training and support to foster carers caring for young people who are approaching adulthood. Arrangements are consistent with the young person's care plan, including their placement plan, pathway plan and transition plan for children with disabilities and special educational needs.

12.4 The fostering service has a policy and practical arrangements which enable children to remain with their foster carer(s) into legal adulthood, for example so that s/he may develop appropriate life skills before being required to move to more independent accommodation. Any such decisions are agreed with foster carers at a placement meeting and are detailed in a child's placement plan.

The above standards are not required for short breaks.

RECRUITMENT AND ASSESSMENT OF FOSTER CARERS

2011 standards	Related 2002 standard	What's new? What's changed?
Standard 13 Recruiting and assessing foster carers who can meet the needs of looked after children	16.12 Administrative procedures are appropriate for dealing promptly with enquiries from prospective carers and any new request for services.	*This standard emphasises the need for transparent and purposeful recruitment and assessment processes for prospective foster carers. The preparatory aspect of the assessment process is highlighted in this standard.*

13.1 The local authority fostering service implements an effective strategy to ensure sufficient foster carers to be responsive to current and predicted future demands on the service. Planning for future demands covers the need for short breaks for disabled children.

13.2 People who are interested in becoming foster carers are treated fairly, without prejudice, openly and with respect. Enquiries are dealt with courteously and efficiently by staff who have the necessary knowledge and skills. Prospective foster carers are provided with timely and relevant information following their initial enquiry and are kept informed about the progress of any subsequent application for approval.

13.3. Prospective foster carers are prepared to become foster carers in a way which addresses, and gives practical techniques to manage, the issues they are likely to encounter and identifies the competencies and strengths they have or need to develop.

13.4 The assessment process is set out clearly to prospective foster carers, including:

a the qualities, skills or aptitudes being sought or to be achieved;
b the standards to be applied in the assessment;
c the stages and content of the selection process and where possible timescales involved;
d the information to be given to applicants.

17.1 The fostering service has an adequate number of sufficiently experienced and qualified staff and recruits a range of carers to meet the needs of children and young people for whom it aims to provide a service.

[17.2 and 17.3 relate to staffing]

17.4 Staff policies encourage retention of salaried staff – including training, regular supervision, study leave, clear workloads and terms and conditions – and of carers by providing support, training and services.

17.5 The fostering service has a recruitment policy and strategy aimed at recruiting a range of carers to meet the needs of children and young people for whom it aims to provide a service.

17.6 There is a clearly set out assessment process for carers which defines:

- task to be undertaken;
- qualities, competences or aptitudes being sought or to be achieved;
- standards to be applied in the assessment;
- stages and content of the selection process and the timescales involved;
- information to be given to applicants.

Linked with the recent emphasis upon 'sufficiency' (see *Sufficiency: Statutory guidance on securing sufficient accommodation for looked after children*, DCSF, 2010), there is greater emphasis upon strategically assessing, and responding to, need.

- New mention of the need to recruit short breaks provision for disabled children (13.1).

- New emphasis upon giving practical techniques as a part of preparation of foster carers and identifying their development needs (13.3), two aspects of the assessment process not cited in the 2002 standards.

- New expectation that the reason for the checks being carried out is made clear to prospective foster carers (13.3).

- More descriptive expectations about the nature of the assessment report, more clearly placed in the context of the panel recommendation and decision making processes (13.4).

- Beyond demonstrating the capacity to care in a 'safe and responsible way that meets the child's developmental needs' (13.6) there are no proposed assessment criteria in the 2011 standards. The assessment criteria set out in the 2002 standards (2002, 17.7) have not been replaced or revised.

2011 standards	Related 2002 standard	What's new? What's changed?
13.5 Checks are carried out in line with regulation 26 and prospective foster carers understand why identity checks, relationship status and health checks, personal references and enquiries are undertaken about them and why enhanced CRB checks are made on them and adult members of their household.	**17.7** In assessing qualities, competences and aptitudes for fostering, fostering services consider them in relation to the following:	• New emphasis upon the need for foster care reviews to be appropriately robust, and for the supervision of foster carers to tackle performance issues and support needs in a timely way (13.8 and 13.9) *between* reviews.

13.6 Prospective foster carers are considered in terms of their capacity to look after children in a safe and responsible way that meets the child's development needs.

13.7 The written report on the person's suitability to be approved as a foster carer sets out clearly all the information that the fostering panel and decision-maker needs in order to make an objective approval decision. The reports are accurate, up-to-date and include evidence based information that distinguishes between fact, opinion and third party information. The reports are prepared, signed and dated by the social worker who assessed the prospective foster carer and countersigned and dated by the fostering team manager or a team manager of another of the provider's fostering teams.

13.8 Reviews of foster carers' approval are sufficiently thorough to allow the fostering service to properly satisfy itself about their carers' ongoing suitability to foster.

13.9 Areas of concern, or need for additional support, that are identified between reviews are addressed. Such matters identified between reviews are addressed at the time they are identified, where appropriate, rather than waiting for a review.

- child rearing;
- caring for children born to somebody else;
- contact between fostered children and their families;
- helping children make sense of their past;
- sexual boundaries and attitudes;
- awareness of issues around child abuse;
- approaches to discipline;
- awareness of how to promote secure attachments between children and appropriate adults;
- awareness of own motivation for fostering/own needs to be met through the fostering process;
- religion;
- racial/cultural/linguistic issues;
- standard of living and lifestyle;
- health;
- own experience of parenting and being parented;
- own experiences in relation to disability and/or attitudes to disability.

FOSTERING PANEL AND DECISION MAKING

2011 standards	Related 2002 standard	What's new? What's changed?
Standard 14 Fostering panels and the fostering service's decision-maker **14.1** The fostering service implements clear written policies and procedures on recruitment to, and maintenance of, the central list of persons considered by them to be suitable to be members of a fostering panel ("the central list") and on constitution of fostering panels. **14.2** Panel/s provide a quality assurance feedback to the fostering service provider on the quality of reports being presented to panel. **14.3** All necessary information is provided to panel members at least five working days in advance of the panel meeting to enable full and proper consideration. **14.4** The fostering panel makes its recommendation on the suitability of a prospective foster carer within eight months of receipt of the prospective foster carer's application to be assessed. **14.5** Foster carers and prospective foster carers are given the opportunity to attend and be heard at all panel meetings at which their approval is being discussed and to bring a supporter to the panel if they wish. **14.6** Fostering panels have access to medical expertise and legal advice, as required. **14.7** The panel chair ensures written minutes of panel meetings are accurate and clearly cover the key issues and views expressed by panel members and record the reasons for its recommendation.	**30.1** Fostering panels have clear written policies and procedures, which are implemented in practice, about the handling of their functions. **30.2** The written procedures cover decision making when all members of the panel are not in agreement. **30.3** There are requirements about suitability of foster panel members, including Criminal Record Bureau checks. No panel members are allowed to begin work until all checks have been satisfactorily completed. **30.4** Fostering panels have access to medical expertise as required. **30.5** Fostering panels provide a quality assurance function in relation to the assessment process – in particular to monitor and review the work of the assessors; to provide feedback; to identify problems; and to ensure that there is consistency of approach in assessment across the service, that it is fair to all applicants and that it has been completed in a thorough and rigorous way. **30.6** Foster panels receive management information about the outcome of foster carers' annual reviews. **30.7** For local authority panels, the panel monitors the range and type of carers available to the authority in comparison with the needs of children. **30.8** The independent members of the panel include, as far as possible, expertise in education and in child health.	*Although the regulations regarding the establishment and operation of the fostering panel are less prescriptive than before, the standards are far more prescriptive regarding timescales at each stage of the panel and decision making processes.* ● Significant change in the form of a potentially limitless 'central list' from which panel membership is drawn. Issues of quorum and tenure are addressed in regulations 23 and 24. The constitution and conduct of the panel are addressed in the statutory guidance paragraphs 5.1 to 5.25. ● The quality assurance function set out in the 2002 standards in relation to *assessments* (2002, 30.5) is now extended to include *all* reports presented to the panel (14.2). ● New expectation that papers are circulated **at least five working days** prior to the panel meeting (14.3). ● New timeline that the panel makes its recommendation within **eight months** of the application (14.4). ● New expectations that panel attendance is always offered to foster carers and applicants, along with a 'supporter' (14.5). ● New mention of access to *legal* advice 'as required' (14.6).

2011 standards	Related 2002 standard	What's new? What's changed?
14.8 The number, skills, knowledge and experience of persons on the central list are sufficient to enable the fostering service to constitute panels that are equipped to make competent recommendations to the fostering service provider, taking into account the nature of the children and carers that the service caters for. 14.9 The fostering service provider's decision-maker makes a considered decision that takes account of all the information available to them, including the recommendation of the fostering panel and, where applicable, the independent review panel, within seven working days of receipt of the recommendation and final set of panel minutes. 14.10 The foster carer or prospective foster carer is informed orally of the decision-maker's decision within two working days and written confirmation is sent to them within five working days.	30.9 One of the independent members is normally a person who has at any time been placed with foster carers or whose child has at any time been placed with foster carers.	● The 2002 emphasis upon educational expertise (2002, 30.8) has been dropped from the 2011 standards, although it is specifically referred to as a potentially useful area of expertise for a panel in paragraph 5.8 of the statutory guidance. ● New specifications regarding the minutes (14.7). ● Less detailed prescription about the membership of the panel (2002, 30.8 and 30.9); instead, reference is made to 'sufficient' membership to make 'competent' recommendations in the context of the service (14.8). ● New expectations of the agency decision-maker, including taking account of *all* the information available and making the decision within **seven working days** of receiving the recommendation (14.9). ● New expectation that the decision will be conveyed orally within **two working days** and confirmed in writing within **five working days**.

MATCHING

2011 standards	Related 2002 standard	What's new? What's changed?
Standard 15 Matching the child with a placement that meets their assessed needs **15.1** The fostering service only suggests foster carers to local authorities as a potential match for a child if the foster carer can reasonably be expected to meet the child's assessed needs and the impact of the placement on existing household members has been considered. Where gaps are identified, the fostering service should work with the responsible authority to ensure the placement plan sets out any additional training, resource or support required. **15.2** Prior to the placement of each child, the foster carer is provided with all the information held by the fostering service that they need to carry out their role effectively. The information is provided in a clear, comprehensive written form and includes the support that will be available to the foster carer. The fostering service follows up with the responsible authority any gaps in the information provided to them on the child or the child's family, which may hinder the foster carer in providing a safe caring environment that meets the child's needs and enables them to keep the child, other children in the fostering household and the foster carer him/herself safe.	**8.1** Local authority fostering services, and voluntary agencies placing children in their own right, ensure that each child or young person placed in foster care is carefully matched with a carer capable of meeting her/his assessed needs. For agencies providing foster carers to local authorities, those agencies ensure that they offer carers only if they represent appropriate matches for a child for whom a local authority is seeking a carer. **8.2** In matching children with carers, responsible authorities take into account the child's care plan and recent written assessments of the child and their family and the carers. **8.3** Matches are achieved by means of information sharing and consideration involving all relevant professionals, the child and her/his family and potential carers, their families and other children in placement. **8.4** Written foster placement agreements contain specific reference to elements of matching which were taken into consideration in agreeing the placement and identify areas where foster carers need additional support to compensate for any gaps in the match between the child and carer. **8.5** Placement decisions consider the child's assessed racial, ethnic, religious, cultural and linguistic needs and match these as closely as possible with the ethnic origin, race, religion, culture and language of the foster family.	*There are no longer any references to "race and culture" in relation to matching within this standard. The emphasis upon seeking full information about the child is even more closely linked to supporting the role of the foster carer than before.* ● Any gaps identified through the matching process are addressed through 'training, resource or support' (15.1) rather than the 'additional support' cited in the 2002 standards (2002, 8.4). ● There is a greater expectation placed upon the fostering service to follow up any shortfalls in the information provided by the responsible authority (15.2), echoing the requirements set out in relation to behaviour management (3.9). ● New presumption of continuity of care in placement, unless the move is in the child's best interests (15.3), reflecting the principles of the Care Planning Regulations 2010. ● New expectation that the responsible authority is notified of any emergency moves within one working day (15.3). ● The emphasis upon matching the child's racial, ethnic, religious, cultural and linguistic needs (2002, 8.5), and the actions to be taken when this is not achieved (2002, 8.6) have gone.

2011 standards	Related 2002 standard	What's new? What's changed?
15.3 Once placed, a child is not removed from a foster carer who is willing and able to continue caring for the child, unless that is in their best interests, taking the child's current wishes and feelings into account, and decided (other than in an emergency) through the child's care planning process. If a placement move occurs in an emergency the fostering service informs the responsible authority within one working day.	8.6 Where transracial or transcommunity placements are made, the responsible authority provides the foster family with additional training, support and information to enable the child to be provided with the best possible care and to develop a positive understanding of her/his heritage. [8.7 addressed in 'Preparing for a Placement' outcome area above.]	

STATEMENT OF PURPOSE AND CHILDREN'S GUIDE

2011 standards	Related 2002 standard	What's new? What's changed?
Standard 16 Statement of purpose and children's guide **16.1** The fostering service has a clear statement of purpose which is available to, and understood by, foster carers, staff and children and is reflected in any policies, procedures and guidance. It is available to the responsible authority and any parent or person with parental responsibility. **16.2** The aims and objectives of the Statement of Purpose are child focused and show how the service will meet outcomes for children. **16.3** Subject to the child's age and understanding, the fostering service ensures the child receives the Children's Guide at the point of placement and that the foster carer explains the contents of the Children's Guide in a way that is accessible. **16.4** The Children's Guide includes a summary of what the fostering service sets out to do for children, how they can find out their rights, how a child can contact their Independent Reviewing Officer, the Children's Rights Director, Ofsted if they wish to raise a concern with inspectors, and how to secure access to an independent advocate. **16.5** Where a child requires it, the guide is available, where appropriate, through suitable alternative methods of communication, e.g. Makaton, pictures, tape recording, translation into another language.	**1.1** There is a clear statement of the aims and objectives of the fostering service and of what facilities and services they provide. **1.2** A statement of purpose clearly sets out what services are provided for children who are placed by the fostering service. If education or health services, including therapeutic services, are provided, these are covered in the statement of purpose. **1.3** The registered provider [in the case of a local authority, the elected members] formally approves the statement of purpose of the fostering service, and reviews, updates and modifies it where necessary at least annually. **1.4** The statement includes details in respect of the fostering services of: • its status and constitution (for agencies); • its management structure; • the services it provides; • its aims and objectives, principles and standards of care; • numbers, relevant qualifications and experience of staff; • numbers of foster carers; • numbers of children placed; • numbers of complaints and their outcomes; • the procedures and processes for recruiting, approving, training, supporting and reviewing carers.	***This standard moves away from detailed prescription regarding content to an expectation that these two core documents are sufficiently accessible to convey what the fostering service aims to achieve.*** • New expectation within the *standards* that the Statement of Purpose is 'available to, and understood by' foster carers, staff and children (16.1), although the more modest expectation to make it available 'upon request' is familiar from the *regulations*. • New emphasis upon demonstrating how outcomes will be achieved in the Statement of Purpose (16.2) rather than describing services (2002, 1.2). • Although the reference in the 2002 standards to review the Statement of Purpose annually (2002, 1.3) has been dropped in the 2011 standards, the regulatory expectation of regular review (regulation 4) remains, and is specified further as being carried out 'at least' annually in the statutory guidance (paragraphs 4.1 to 4.4). • Far less prescription about the contents of the Statement of Purpose. The detailed requirements previously set out (2002, 1.4) have not been revised or replaced although the statutory guidance does now demand specific reference to parent and child placements when a fostering service offers this type of provision (statutory guidance paragraph 1.13).

2011 standards	Related 2002 standard	What's new? What's changed?
	1.5 The children's guide to the fostering service is suitable for all children fostered through the service, includes a summary of what the service sets out to do for children, and is provided to children as soon as they are fostered, and to all foster carers. (If necessary, the guide is produced in different formats to meet the needs of different groups of children.) The children's guide contains information on how a child can secure access to an independent advocate and about how to complain. 1.6 The fostering service's policies, procedures and any written guidance to staff and carers accurately reflect the statement of purpose.	• New expectation that the foster carer explains the children's guide to the child 'in a way that is accessible' (16.3). • New emphasis upon children's rights in the Children's Guide allied to the requirement to inform children how to contact their IRO, the Children's Rights Director and Ofsted (16.4). • More examples offered regarding the provision of alternative formats of the Children's Guide (16.5). See also standard 30.2 below regarding friends and family carers.

MANAGEMENT AND ADMINISTRATION

2011 standards	Related 2002 standard	What's new? What's changed?
Standard 17 Fitness to provide or manage the administration of a fostering service	2.1 The people involved in carrying on and managing the fostering service possess the necessary business and management skills and financial expertise to manage the work efficiently and effectively and have the necessary knowledge and experience of child care and fostering to do so in a professional manner.	*This standard contains important changes to the timing and level of the management qualifications required.*

<table>
<tr><td>

17.1 People involved in carrying on and managing the fostering service:

a have good knowledge and experience of law and practice relating to looked after children;

b have business and management skills to manage the work efficiently and effectively; and

c have financial expertise to ensure that the fostering service is run on a sound financial basis and in a professional manner.

17.2 The registered manager (or registered person, where the registered person is an individual and there is no registered manager) has:

a a recognised social work qualification or a professional qualification relevant to working with children at least at level 4;

b a qualification in management at least at level 4[1];

c at least two years' experience relevant to fostering within the last five years; and

d at least one year's experience supervising and managing professional staff.

17.3 Appointees to the role of registered manager who do not have the management qualification (above) must enrol on a management training course within six months, and obtain a relevant management qualification within three years, of their appointment.

</td><td>

2.2 The manager has:

a professional qualification relevant to working with children, which must be either NVQ level 4 or the DipSW or another qualification that matches the competencies required by the NVQ Level 4;

by 2005, a qualification at level 4 NVQ in management or another qualification which matches the competencies required by the NVQ Level 4; and

at least two years' experience of working with children within the past five years, and in addition at least one year's experience of working at a senior level.

2.3 For the transitional period in relation to management qualifications, appointees to the post of manager who have no such qualifications begin appropriate management training within six months of appointment.

2.4 The manager exercises effective leadership of the staff and operation, such that the fostering service is organised, managed and staffed in a manner that delivers the best possible child care.

</td><td>

- New expectation that those *embarking* on the process to achieve a relevant management qualification now seek NVQ Level 5, not 4. Those who already hold a Level 4 relevant management qualification need not seek qualification to Level 5 (17.2b).

- New expectation that those without a relevant management qualification must *achieve* one **within three years** of appointment (17.3) rather than *beginning* the process within 6 months set out in the 2002 standards (2002, 2.3).

- The expectation to have 'worked with children' for two years of the last five in the 2002 standards is now altered to experience 'relevant to fostering' (17.2b).

- New focus in this context that the manager remains clear about their duties and to whom they are accountable (17.4).

</td></tr>
</table>

1   With respect to standard 17.2 (a) and (b), for persons undertaking a qualification after January 2011, the relevant qualification will be the Level 5 Diploma in Leadership for Health and Social Care and Children and Young People's Services. Managers who already hold a Level 4 Leadership and Management for Care Service and Health and Social Care will not need to undertake this qualification at Level 5.

2011 standards	Related 2002 standard	What's new? What's changed?
17.4 The responsibilities and duties of the manager, and to whom they are accountable, are clear and understood by them. The manager is notified in writing of any change in the person to whom they are accountable.		
17.5 The manager exercises effective leadership of the staff and operation, such that the fostering service is organised, managed and staffed in a manner that delivers the best possible child care that meets the individual needs of each fostered child and of foster carers.		

FINANCIAL VIABILITY

2011 standards	Related 2002 standard	What's new? What's changed?
Standard 18 Financial viability and changes affecting business continuity **18.1** A qualified accountant certifies that the independent fostering agency's annual accounts indicate the service is financially viable and likely to have sufficient funding to continue to fulfil its Statement of Purpose for at least the next 12 months. **18.2** The registered provider has a written development plan, reviewed annually, for the future of the service, either identifying any planned changes in the operation or resources of the service, or confirming the continuation of the service's current operation and resource. **18.3** Where the service, for any reason, cannot adequately and consistently maintain provision which complies with regulations or NMS, an effective plan must be established and implemented either to rectify the situation or to close down the service. **18.4** The registered provider must notify Ofsted, the responsible authority and where different the placing authority if closure of the service or substantial change to the service significantly affecting the care, welfare or placement of children, is likely or actively being considered. The registered person should work with the responsible authority/placing authority to ensure as smooth a transition for children and foster carers as possible.	**4.3** The service has proper financial procedures and there is a reviewing procedure to keep them up to date. **27.1** The agency ensures it is financially viable at all times and has sufficient financial resources to fulfil its obligations. **27.2** Procedures exist to deal with situations of financial crisis, such as disclosing information to purchasers and liaising with them to safeguard the welfare of children receiving services through the agency. **27.3** Regulations and guidelines imposed upon businesses are conformed with. This includes Income Tax (PAYE), National Insurance and VAT. **28.1** The financial processes/systems of the agency are properly operated and maintained in accordance with sound and appropriate accounting standards and practice. **28.2** The agency has clearly documented financial arrangements for control andsupervision of its financial affairs and powers. **28.3** The agency has a clearly written set of principles and standards governing its financial management and these are communicated to its managers and accountants. **28.4** The agency has a written set of principles describing the financial procedures and responsibilities to be followed by all staff, consultants, professional experts, directors, trustees and any manager. **28.5** The agency's accounts are maintained and properly audited by a registered accountant. **28.6** The registered provider regularly receives information on the financial state of the agency.	*The desire to provide security and stability for children is evident in this standard's commitment to 'early warning systems' for any financial difficulties.* ● Although the 2002 regulation 43 required accountancy oversight (retained in the 2011 regulation 37), the expectation to provide formal assurance about the forthcoming year is a subtle but significant change (18.1). ● New expectation to have an annually reviewed 'written development plan' (18.2). ● New expectations when the agency cannot continue to operate within the National Minimum Standards (18.3) including the transfer of records in the event of closure (18.5). ● New expectation to notify Ofsted of any anticipated 'substantial' changes that may have an impact upon children. (18.4). This pre-empts the regulatory requirements regarding bankruptcy and the appointment of liquidators. ● New expectation to have regard for the needs of children and foster carers in the event of administration or receivership (18.6).

2011 standards	Related 2002 standard	What's new? What's changed?
18.5 Any person or organisation temporarily responsible for a fostering service in administration or receivership, or in the process of closure or substantial change, must operate the service in the best interests of the placed children and foster carers under the circumstances that apply, in accordance with the applicable regulations and these standards.	28.7 The agency publishes its charges for each of its services and has a clear policy for the charging of fees and expenses for any additional services it is asked to provide. The statement is available on request to purchasers and others with a legitimate interest.	

SUITABILITY TO WORK WITH CHILDREN

2011 standards	Related 2002 standard	What's new? What's changed?
Standard 19 Suitability to work with children **19.1** All people working in or for the fostering service and the central list of persons considered suitable to be members of a fostering panel are interviewed as part of the selection process and have references checked to assess suitability before taking on responsibilities. Telephone enquiries are made to each referee to verify the written references.[1] **19.2** The fostering service can demonstrate, including from written records, that it consistently follows good recruitment practice, and all applicable current statutory requirements and guidance, in foster carer selection and staff and panel member recruitment. This includes CRB checks.[2] All personnel responsible for recruitment and selection of staff are trained in, understand and operate these good practices. **19.3** The fostering service has a record of the recruitment and suitability checks which have been carried out for foster carers and those working (including as volunteers) for the fostering service which includes: **a** identity checks; **b** CRB Disclosures, including the level of the Disclosure and the unique reference number (in line with eligibility to obtain such checks);	**15.1** Any people working in or for the fostering service are suitable people to work with children and young people and to safeguard and promote their welfare. **15.2** There are clear written recruitment and selection procedures for appointing staff which follow good practice in safeguarding children and young people. All personnel responsible for recruitment and selection of staff are trained in, understand and operate these. **15.3** All people working in or for the fostering service are interviewed as part of the selection process and have references checked to assess suitability before taking on responsibilities. Telephone enquiries are made as well as obtaining written references. **15.4** Records are kept of checks and references that have been obtained and their outcomes. Police checks are renewed every three years. **18.7** There is a whistle blowing policy which is made known to all staff and carers.	*This standard sets out in detail the checks required of staff and panel members. Although some elements remain from the 2002 standards – such as the telephone confirmation of references – other expectations in terms of required checks are more detailed than before. Given anticipated changes to vetting and barring arrangements we can expect some further amendments to this standard.* ● Greater detail regarding the records to be held in relation to the recruitment process for all working 'in or for' the fostering service (19.3). ● Specific reference to potential 'further checks' when recruiting someone who has worked outside the UK (19.3(f)). ● More detail regarding the retention and disposal of CRB disclosures (19.4). The reference to renewal every three years in the 2002 standards (2002, 15.4) has gone.

1   These requirements are the responsibility of Ofsted with respect to checking suitability of those seeking to carry on or manage a fostering service.

2   Please note that the Government is currently reviewing the criminal records system and vetting and barring scheme and therefore references in both the regulations and standards may be subject to change.

2011 standards	Related 2002 standard	What's new? What's changed?
c checks to confirm qualifications which are a requirement and those that are considered by the fostering service to be relevant; d at least two references, preferably one from a current employer, and where possible a statement from each referee as to their opinion of the person's suitability to work with children; e checks to confirm the right to work in the UK; f where the person has lived outside of the UK, further checks, as are considered appropriate, where obtaining a CRB Disclosure is not sufficient to establish suitability to work with children. 19.4 The record must show the date on which each check was completed and who carried out the check. The CRB Disclosure information must be kept in secure conditions and be destroyed by secure means as soon as it is no longer needed in line with the CRB Code of Practice. Before the Disclosure is destroyed, records need to be kept as described above. 19.5 The registered person's system for recruiting staff and others includes an effective system for reaching decisions as to who is to be appointed and the circumstances in which an application should be refused in the light of any criminal convictions or other concerns about suitability that are declared or discovered through the recruitment process. 19.6 There is a whistle-blowing policy which is made known to all staff, volunteers, foster carers and panel members. This makes it a clear duty for such people to report to an appropriate authority any circumstances within the fostering service which they consider likely to significantly harm the safety, rights or welfare of any child placed by the service.		• Of note, the current CRB Code of Practice accepts the secure retention of the CRB until the next inspection as follows: 'To note: those Registered Care Homes which are inspected by the Care Quality Commission (CQC), those organisations which are inspected by Ofsted and those establishments which are inspected by the Care and Social Services Inspectorate for Wales (CSSIW) may retain the Certificate until the next inspection. Once the inspection has taken place the Certificate should be destroyed in accordance with the CRB Code of Practice.' • More explicit expectations regarding the decision making process relating to those with criminal convictions (19.5). • More description regarding the components of a whistle-blowing policy (19.6), including who needs to be aware of it, now extended to include volunteers and panel members.

TRAINING FOR FOSTER CARERS

2011 standards	Related 2002 standard	What's new? What's changed?
Standard 20 Learning and development of foster carers	23.1 The fostering service ensures that foster carers are trained in the skills required to provide high quality care and meet the needs of each child/young person placed in their care.	*This standard takes account of the development of the Training, Support and Development Standards for Foster Care. This standard promotes the principle that all foster carers have ongoing learning and development needs that services need to monitor and address.*
20.1 All new foster carers receive an induction.		
20.2 All foster carers, including all members of a household who are approved foster carers, are supported to achieve the Children's Workforce Development Council's Training, Support and Development Standards for Foster Care. Short break carers who are approved foster carers are supported to achieve the Training Support & Development Standards for Short Break Carers. Family and friends foster carers are supported to achieve the Training, Support and Development Standards for Family and Friends Foster Carers.[2]	23.2 Pre-approval and induction training for each carer includes opportunities to benefit from the experience and knowledge of existing carers. All new foster carers receive induction training.	● New expectation to provide induction for all carers (20.1).
	23.3 All training fits within a framework of equal opportunities, anti-discriminatory practice and is organised to encourage and facilitate attendance by foster carers, for example by including convenient times and venues and by providing childcare and reasonable expenses.	● New expectation to support the achievement of the Children's Workforce Development Council's (CWDC) Training, Support and Development Standards (and short breaks equivalent) (20.2).
20.3 Foster carers are able to evidence that the Training, Support and Development Standards have been attained within 12 months of approval (or within 18 months for family and friends foster carers). For foster carers who were approved as such before April 2008, the standards are attained by April 2011 (or by April 2012 for family and friends foster carers). Fostering households may use the same evidence workbook.	23.4 Where two adults in one household are approved as joint carers, both successfully complete all training. Each foster carer is trained in identified key areas prior to any child being placed in his or her home. Attention is given to the training needs of particular groups, e.g. male carers.	● New expectation that foster carers attain the CWDC Standards **within 12 months of approval** and **within 18 months for friends and family carers**, with specific dates for those previously approved (20.3).
		● Acknowledgement that two foster carers in the same households can use the same CWDC workbook (20.3).
20.4 Foster carers maintain an ongoing training and development portfolio which demonstrates how they are meeting the skills required of them by the fostering service.	23.5 There is an ongoing programme of training and self-development for foster carers to develop their skills and tackle any weaknesses.	● Building upon annual appraisal of training provided in the 2002 standards (2002, 23.8), new expectation that each foster carer has a personal development plan (20.5) reviewed at each annual review (20.6).
	23.6 Appropriate training on safe caring is provided for all members of the foster household.	
20.5 Foster carers' personal development plans set out how they will be supported to undertake ongoing training and development that is appropriate to their development needs and experience.	23.7 Specific consideration is given to any help or support needed by the sons and daughters of foster carers.	● New emphasis upon clarity regarding the support to be offered to foster carers (20.7).
	23.8 Each carer's Annual Review includes an appraisal of training and development needs, which is documented in the review report.	● New concept of 'hard to reach' carers along with expectation of additional measures to engage them (20.8).

1 For information and guidance please visit www.cwdcouncil.org.uk/foster-care/standards.

2 Short break carers/family and friends carers may choose to undertake the mainstream Training, Support and Development Standards for Foster Care, instead of the Standards for Short Break Carers/Family and Friends Carers, if this is their preference.

2011 standards	Related 2002 standard	What's new? What's changed?
20.6 The reviews of each carer's approval include an appraisal of performance against clear and consistent standards set by the agency, and consideration of training and development needs, which are documented in the review report. The foster carer's personal development plan is reviewed and the effectiveness of training and development received is evaluated. Reviews take into account the views of each child currently placed with the foster carer.	**23.9** The effectiveness of training received is evaluated and reviewed annually.	• New expectation that training portfolios will be made available upon request when foster carers move between agencies (20.11).
20.7 The fostering service is clear and transparent with their foster carers about the level of support available to them and how to access such support.		
20.8 Support and training is made available to foster carers, including hard to reach carers,[3] to assist them in meeting the specific needs of the children they are caring for or are expected to care for.		
20.9 Appropriate training on safer caring is provided for all members of the foster household, including young people of sufficient age and understanding, and ensures that foster carers understand how safer caring principles should be applied in a way which meets the needs of individual children.		
20.10 All training fits within a framework of equal opportunities and anti-discriminatory practice and is organised to encourage and facilitate attendance by foster carers.		
20.11 In cases where a foster carer moves to a new fostering service, details of the development and training which he or she has undertaken, and of the extent to which the agreed training and development standards have been met, are made available on request to the new provider, and the foster carer is able to take their training and development portfolio with them.		

---

3 www.cwdcouncil.org.uk/foster-care/case-studies/reaching-all-carers provides helpful case studies.

FOSTER CARER SUPERVISION

2011 standards	Related 2002 standard	What's new? What's changed?
Standard 21 Supervision and support of foster carers **21.1.** The fostering service supports their foster carers to ensure they provide foster children with care that reasonably meets those children's needs, takes the children's wishes and feelings into account, actively promotes individual care and supports the children's safety, health, enjoyment, education and preparation for the future. **21.2** The fostering service ensures foster carers understand the nature and level of support which will be provided to them by the fostering service. **21.3** There is an effective out of hours advice and support service for foster carers. **21.4** Peer support, foster care associations and/or self-help groups for foster carers are encouraged and supported. **21.5** Foster carers are provided with breaks from caring as appropriate. These are planned to take account of the needs of any children placed. **21.6** All foster carers have access to adequate social work and other professional support, information and advice, to enable them to provide consistent, high quality care to the child. This includes assistance with dealing with relevant services, such as health and education. Consideration is given to any help or support needed by the sons and daughters of foster carers. **21.7** The role of the supervising social worker is clear both to the worker and the foster carer.	**16.15** All fostering service social workers understand the role of the children's social workers, and there is a clear understanding about how the fostering service social workers and the children's social workers work effectively together. **18.3** Out of hours management and support services are available for foster carers. **18.4** There are management systems for carer supervision, appraisal and support. **21.1** The fostering service has a clear strategy for working with and supporting carers. **21.2** There is a clear strategy for working with carers that is documented and understood. This includes: ● arrangements for training and development; ● encouragement for self-help groups; ● supervision; ● support services; ● *information and advice;* ● assistance in dealing with other relevant services, such as health and education; ● out-of-hours support; ● respite care; ● arrangements for reviews.	*This standard draws together a number of different standards in the 2002 version. Supervision is consistently linked in this standard to ensuring good outcomes for foster children.* ● New emphasis upon foster carers understanding the level of support made available to them (21.2), using very similar wording to 20.7. ● New emphasis upon *peer support* (21.4) in addition to the replication of the references to support groups and foster care associations made in the 2002 standards (2002, 21.2 and 2002, 22.7). ● The provision of 'respite care' for foster carers in the 2002 standards (2002, 21.2 and 2002, 22.7) is now described as 'breaks from caring' in the 2011 standards, 'if appropriate' and taking 'account of the needs of any children placed' (21.5). ● Specific reference now made to the birth children of foster carers (21.6). ● The specific reference to supporting foster carers to deal with health and education services echoes and underpins the advocacy role sought from foster carers on these areas in standards 6 and 8 (21.6). ● The new standards provide a far fuller description of the areas to be covered in the good quality supervision of foster carers, including a focus upon the child's wishes and feelings linked to the foster carers' ongoing learning and development (21.8).

2011 standards	Related 2002 standard	What's new? What's changed?
21.8 Each approved foster carer is supervised by a named, appropriately qualified social worker who has meetings with the foster carer, including at least one unannounced visit a year. Meetings have a clear purpose and provide the opportunity to supervise the foster carer's work, ensure the foster carer is meeting the child's needs, taking into account the child's wishes and feelings, and offer support and a framework to assess the carer's performance and develop their competencies and skills. The frequency of meetings for short break foster carers should be proportionate to the amount of care provided. Foster carers' files include records of supervisory meetings.	**21.5** The role of the supervising social worker is clear both to the worker and the carer.	• New acknowledgement that the frequency of supervision meetings for short breaks carers should be proportionate to their role (21.8).
	21.6 There is a good system of communication between the fostering service social workers and the child's social worker.	• New focus upon allegation management in the handbook provided to foster carers (21.10).
	22.1 The fostering service is a managed one which provides supervision for foster carers and helps them to develop their skills.	• New emphasis upon potential complaints *by* foster carers and prospective foster carers (21.11).
21.9 The supervising social worker ensures each foster carer he or she supervises is informed in writing of, and accepts, understands and operates within, all regulations and standards and with policies and guidance agreed by the fostering service.	**22.2** Foster care agreements ensure foster carers have a full understanding of what is expected of foster carers, the agency and/or the local authority.	• New *context* for the need for good communication between the supervising social worker and the *child's* social worker from the 2002 standards (2002, 16.15), now linked more clearly with effective foster carer supervision (21.12).
21.10 On approval, foster carers are given information, either a handbook or electronic resources, which cover policies, procedures (including with regard to allegations), guidance, financial information, legal information and insurance details. This information is updated regularly.	**22.3** Each approved foster carer is supervised by a named, appropriately qualified social worker and has access to adequate social work and other professional support, information and advice to enable her or him to provide consistent, high quality care for a child or young person placed in her or his home. The supervising social worker ensures each carer she or he supervises is informed in writing of, and accepts, understands and operates within, all standards, policies and guidance agreed by the fostering service.	
21.11 Current and prospective foster carers are able to make a complaint about any aspect of the service which affects them directly. Records are kept of representations and complaints, how they are dealt with, the outcome and any action taken. These records are reviewed regularly so that the service's practice is improved where necessary.	**22.4** In producing the Foster Care Agreement for a foster carer, in line with Schedule 5 of the Fostering Services Regulations 2001, the fostering provider ensures that the Agreement contains the information they need to know, in a comprehensible style, to carry out their functions as a foster carer effectively.	

2011 standards	Related 2002 standard	What's new? What's changed?
21.12 There is a good system of communication between the fostering service social workers and the child's social worker. The fostering service social workers understand the role of the child's social worker and work effectively with them.	22.5 On approval, carers are given a handbook which covers policies, procedures, guidance, legal information and insurance details. This is updated regularly. 22.6 Supervising social workers meet regularly with foster carers. Meetings have a clear purpose and provide the opportunity to supervise the foster carers' work. Foster carers' files include records of supervisory meetings. There are occasional unannounced visits, at least one each year. 22.7 There is a system of practical support for carers, including: ● out of hours management support; ● prompt payment; ● insurance cover; ● support for foster care associations; ● respite care where appropriate; ● access to social work support. 22.8 Information about the procedures for dealing with complaints and representations is widely available. Complaints and representations are recorded and monitored and the outcome evaluated to inform future provision of services.	

ALLEGATION MANAGEMENT

2011 standards	Related 2002 standard	What's new? What's changed?

Standard 22 Handling allegations and suspicions of harm

22.1 All foster carers, fostering service staff and volunteers understand what they must do if they receive an allegation or have suspicions that a person may have:

a behaved in a way that has, or may have, harmed a child;

b possibly committed a criminal offence against or related to a child; or

c behaved towards a child in a way that indicates he or she is unsuitable to work with children.

The fostering service ensures that the required actions are taken, or have been taken, in any relevant situation of which it is aware.

22.2 The fostering service's procedure is in line with Government guidance and requirements, including the duty to refer information to statutory bodies.[1] It is known to foster carers, fostering service staff, volunteers and children.

22.3 A copy of the fostering service provider's child protection procedures is made available to foster carers, fostering service staff, volunteers and children. Any comments on these procedures are taken into account by the provider.

22.9 Information about the procedures to deal with investigations into allegations is made known to foster care staff, carers and children and young people and includes the provision of independent support to the foster carer(s) during an investigation.

22.10 Records about allegations of abuse are kept and monitored and there is a clear policy framework which outlines the circumstances in which a carer should be removed from the foster carer register.

25.13 There is a system for keeping records about allegations and complaints and for handling these confidentially and securely. Records of complaints and allegations are clearly recorded on the relevant files for staff, carers and children – including details of the investigation, conclusion reached and action taken. Separate records are also kept which bring together data on allegations and on complaints.

***Reflecting* Working Together *(DCSF, 2010), nearly all of this standard is new. An important new term, 'concern', is introduced, and greater transparency is demanded in terms of process and payment. See also the statutory guidance paragraphs 3.68 to 3.81.**

- *Working Together* definition of an allegation now incorporated (22.1).

- New emphasis upon ensuring the relevant policy is known to all parties, including children and their comments taken account of (22.2).

- New expectation to submit policies to the LSCB and LADO or equivalent and to ensure they are consistent with the responsible authority (22.4).

- New expectation to have an organisational lead for allegation management in each service (22.5).

- New expectation to report allegations that 'on the face of it may appear relatively insignificant' to the LADO (22.6).

- New recording and retention expectations in line with *Working Together* guidance (22.7).

- Expectation to review the approval of foster carers 'as soon as possible' after the investigation is concluded (22.8).

---

1 Since October 2009, the duties to refer concerns regarding individuals under List 99 and the Protection of Children Act 1999 have been replaced by with a duty to provide information to the Independent Safeguarding Authority. Please see the referrals page of www.isa-gov.org.uk for information on the legal requirements for making referrals.

2011 standards	Related 2002 standard	What's new? What's changed?
22.4 The fostering service provider's child protection procedures are submitted for consideration and comment to the Local Safeguarding Children's Board (LSCB) and to the Local Authority Designated Officer (LADO) for Child Protection[2] (or other senior officer responsible for child protection matters in that department). They are consistent with the local policies and procedures agreed by the LSCB relevant to the geographical area where the foster carer lives. Any conflicts between locally agreed procedures and those of other placing authorities are discussed and resolved as far as possible. **22.5** Each fostering service has a designated person, who is a senior manager, responsible for managing allegations. The designated person has responsibility for liaising with the LADO and for keeping the subject of the allegation informed of progress during and after the investigation. **22.6** Allegations against people that work with children or members of the fostering household are reported by the fostering service to the LADO. This includes allegations that on the face of it may appear relatively insignificant or that have also been reported directly to the police or Children and Family Services.		• This sense of urgency is also reflected in the timescales set out in the statutory guidance: if no formal action is required, 'appropriate action' should be instituted within 3 working days; if further action is required 'without further investigation, this should be done within 15 working days' (Statutory guidance paragraph 3.81). • New distinction between allegations and concerns regarding standard of care (22.10). • New clarity required regarding payment of allowance and fee during investigations (22.11). See also standard 2.85. • Greater detail about the nature of the independent support to be offered to foster carers during an investigation (22.12). • Although not specifically addressed in the standards themselves, the statutory guidance emphasises the need to maintain the confidentiality of the person subject of an allegation during the investigation process (paragraph 3.77), reflecting recent debates about allegation management in schools. • Further important guidance outlining that unfounded allegations should not be referred to in references is contained in paragraph 3.79 of the statutory guidance.

2 *Working Together to Safeguard Children* (DCSF, 2010).

2011 standards	Related 2002 standard	What's new? What's changed?

22.7 A clear and comprehensive summary of any allegations made against a particular member of the fostering household, or staff member, including details of how the allegation was followed up and resolved, a record of any action taken and the decisions reached, is kept on the person's confidential file. A copy is provided to the person as soon as the investigation is concluded. The information is retained on the confidential file, even after someone leaves the organisation, until the person reaches normal retirement age, or for ten years if this is longer.

22.8 As soon as possible after an investigation into a foster carer is concluded, their approval as suitable to foster is reviewed. There is a clear policy framework which outlines the circumstances in which a foster carer should be removed as one of the fostering service provider's approved foster carers, in the interests of the safety or welfare of children. This is available to foster carers.

22.9 Investigations into allegations or suspicions of harm are handled fairly, quickly, and consistently in a way that provides effective protection for the child, and at the same time supports the person who is the subject of the allegation. Fostering services follow the framework for managing cases of allegations of abuse against people who work with children as set out in *Working Together to Safeguard Children*.

2011 standards	Related 2002 standard	What's new? What's changed?
22.10 Fostering services ensure that a clear distinction is made between investigation into allegations of harm and discussions over standards of care. Investigations which find no evidence of harm should not become procedures looking into poor standards of care – these should be treated separately.		
22.11 There is written guidance for foster carers and staff, which makes clear how they will be supported during an investigation into an allegation including payment of allowance and any fee to foster carers while investigations are ongoing.		
22.12 During an investigation the fostering service makes support, which is independent of the fostering service, available to the person subject to the allegation and, where this is a foster carer, to their household, in order to provide: **a** information and advice about the process; **b** emotional support; and, **c** if needed, mediation between the foster carer and the fostering service and/or advocacy (including attendance at meetings and panel hearings).		

TRAINING OF STAFF (AND PANEL MEMBERS)

2011 standards	Related 2002 standard	What's new? What's changed?

Standard 23 Learning, development and qualifications of staff

23.1 There is a good quality learning and development programme, which includes induction, post-qualifying and in-service training, that staff and volunteers are supported to undertake. The programme equips them with the skills required to meet the needs of the children, keeps them up-to-date with professional, legal and practice developments and reflects the policies, legal obligations and business needs of the fostering service.

23.2 The learning and development programme is evaluated for effectiveness at least annually and is updated where necessary.

23.3. New staff and volunteers undertake the Children's Workforce Development Council's induction standards, commencing within 7 working days of starting their employment and being completed within six months.

23.4 All social workers and other specialists (e.g. medical, legal, educationalists, psychologists, therapists) are professionally qualified and, where applicable, registered by the appropriate professional body. They are appropriately trained to work with children, their families and foster carers, and have a good understanding of foster care and the policies and purpose of the fostering service.

23.5 Assessment and appraisal of all staff involved in fostering work takes account of identified skills needed for particular roles and is used to identify individuals' learning and development needs.

15.5 All social work staff have an appropriate qualification, or are in the course of obtaining a suitable professional qualification, to work with children and young people, their families and foster carers, and have a good understanding of foster care. They have appropriate knowledge and skills. These include:

- understanding of the Children Act, the Children Act regulations and guidance, relevant current policies and procedures, *Working Together* and associated child protection guidance, the *Framework for the Assessment of Children in Need and their Families* (DH, 2000), the regulatory requirements under the Care Standards Act 2000 and adoption law;

- knowledge of the growth and development of children and an ability to communicate with children and young people;

- understanding the importance of a complaints procedure;

- an ability to promote equality, diversity and the rights of individuals and groups;

- knowledge of the roles of other agencies, in particular health and education.

15.6 Any social work staff involved in assessment and approval of foster carers are qualified social workers, have experience of foster care and family placement work and are trained in assessment. Students and others who do not meet this requirement carry out assessments and approvals under the supervision of someone who does, who takes responsibility for the assessments and approvals.

This standard sets out greater expectations in terms of training, both for staff members and panel members.

- New expectation to have a learning and development programme for staff and volunteers which is evaluated at least annually (23.2).

- New expectation that all staff and volunteers undertake the CWDC induction standards within seven work days of starting, and complete them within six months (23.3).

- New reference to the 'central list' first cited in standard 14 (23.8).

- New expectation that those joining the 'central list' will be given the opportunity to observe panel prior to joining the list (23.8).

- Note that, although those from the central list need not attend each panel, they are expected to complete an induction within ten weeks of *joining the list*, not within ten weeks of attending their first panel meeting (23.9).

- Expectation of annual joint training involving between panel members and staff (23.10) and greater emphasis upon learning and development of panel members (23.11).

- New criteria for the agency decision-maker, including requirement to be a social worker with at least three years' post-qualifying experience (23.12).

- The emphasis upon the promotion of equality in the 2002 standards (2002, 15.5) has gone.

2011 standards	Related 2002 standard	What's new? What's changed?
23.6 Any staff involved in assessing the suitability of persons to be foster carers are social workers, have experience of foster care and family placement work and are trained in assessment. Social work students and social workers who do not have the relevant experience, only carry out assessments under the supervision of an appropriately experienced social worker, who takes responsibility for the assessment.	15.7 All educationalists, psychologists, therapists and other professional staff are professionally qualified and appropriately trained to work with children and young people, their families and foster carers, and have a good understanding of foster care.	
23.7 Where unqualified staff and volunteers carry out social work functions, they do so under the direct supervision of experienced social workers, who are accountable for their work.	15.8 Where unqualified staff carry out social work functions they do so under the direct supervision of qualified social workers, who are accountable for their work.	
23.8 Persons joining the central list of persons considered suitable to be fostering panel members are provided with an opportunity to observe a fostering panel meeting.	18.3 Out of hours management and support services are available for foster carers.	
23.9 Each person on the central list is given induction training which is completed within 10 weeks of joining the central list.		
23.10 Each person on the central list is given the opportunity of attending an annual joint training day with the fostering service's fostering staff.		
23.11 Each person on the central list has access to appropriate training and skills development and is kept abreast of relevant changes to legislation and guidance.		
23.12 The fostering service's decision-maker is a senior person within the fostering service, or is a trustee or director of the fostering service, who is a social worker with at least 3 years post-qualifying experience in childcare social work and has knowledge of childcare law and practice.		

STAFF SUPERVISION

2011 standards	Related 2002 standard	What's new? What's changed?
Standard 24 Staff support and supervision 24.1 The employer is fair and competent, with sound employment practices and good support for all its staff and volunteers. 24.2 All staff, volunteers and the registered person are properly managed and supported and understand to whom they are accountable. 24.3 Suitable arrangements exist for professional supervision of the agency's registered person or manager of a local authority fostering service. 24.4. Staff have access to support and advice, and are provided with regular supervision by appropriately qualified and experienced staff. 24.5 A written record is kept by the fostering service detailing the time, date and length of each supervision held for each member of staff, including the registered person. The record is signed by the supervisor and the member of staff at the end of the supervision. 24.6 All staff have their performance individually and formally appraised at least annually and, where they are working with children, this appraisal takes into account any views of children the service is providing for. 24.7 Staff and volunteers are able to access the specialist advice needed to provide a comprehensive service for children, including legal advice.	18.1 The fostering service is a fair and competent employer, with sound employment practices and good support for its staff and carers. 18.2 There are sound employment practices, in relation to both staff and carers. [18.3 and 18.4 now addressed within foster carer supervision outcome area.] [18.5 now addressed within physical environment outcome.] 18.6 For agencies, there is a public liability and professional indemnity insurance for all staff and carers. The insurance policy covers costs arising as a result of child abuse claims against any staff or carers. [18.7 Whistle-blowing now addressed under 'Suitability to work with children' outcome area.] 20.1 All staff are properly accountable and supported. 20.2 All staff have clear written details of the duties and responsibilities expected of them, together with the policies and procedures of the organisation. 20.3 All staff who come into contact with foster carers and prospective foster carers and children/young people receive management supervision and a record is kept by the line manager of the content of the supervision and of progress made. Supervision sessions are regular and planned in advance. 20.4 Staff receive regular, planned appraisals from their line manager. 20.5 Each member of staff has the opportunity to attend regular staff and team meetings.	*This standard sets out more specific expectations in terms of supervision, particularly in relation to supervision records. These responsibilities are now extended to volunteers.* ● New application of employment and support practices to *volunteers* (24.1) (24.2) (24.7). ● New expectations regarding the detail of the information to be included in staff supervision records: (24.5). ● New expectation that supervision records with staff are signed by both parties 'at the end of the supervision' (24.5). ● New expectation that the views of children are taken into account when appraising staff who work directly with them (24.6). ● Echoing the advice proposed for the fostering panel (14.6), there is a new emphasis upon legal advice (24.7). ● The reference in the 2002 standards to professional indemnity (2002, 18.6) is not in the 2011 standards. ● There is no longer any reference to team meetings (2002, 20.5).

MANAGEMENT AND MONITORING

2011 standards	Related 2002 standard	What's new? What's changed?
Standard 25 Managing effectively and efficiently and monitoring the service 25.1 There are clear and effective procedures for monitoring and controlling the activities of the service. This includes the financial viability of the service, any serious incidents, allegations or complaints about the service and ensuring the quality of the service. 25.2 The manager regularly monitors all records kept by the service to ensure compliance with the service's policies, to identify any concerns about specific incidents and to identify patterns and trends. Immediate action is taken to address any issues raised by this monitoring. 25.3 Management of the service ensures all staff's work and all fostering activity is consistent with the 2011 regulations and NMS and with the service's policies and procedures. 25.4 Managers, staff, volunteers and foster carers are clear about their roles and responsibilities. The level of delegation and responsibility of the manager, and the lines of accountability, are clearly defined. 25.5 Clear arrangements are in place to identify the person in charge when the registered manager, or local authority fostering service manager, is absent. 25.6 The registered person ensures copies of inspection reports by Ofsted are made available to all members of staff, to their foster carers, children fostered by the service and their parents/carers, and, on request, to responsible or where different placing authorities of existing foster children or those considering placing a child through the service.	4.1 There are clear procedures for monitoring and controlling the activities of the fostering service and ensuring quality performance. 4.2 There are clear roles for managers and staff and well established lines of communication and of accountability between managers, staff and carers. [4.3 regarding financial viability now address in 'Financial Viability Outcome' area above.] 4.4 Information is provided to purchasers of services and others. This includes: • charges for each of its services; • statements of the amounts paid to foster carers; and • itemised amounts paid for wider services which may include health and education. 4.5 The fostering service informs carers, managers and staff of their responsibility to declare any possible conflicts of interest. 5.1 The fostering service is managed effectively and efficiently. 5.2 The manager has a clear job description setting out duties and responsibilities and does not hold a similar position in another organisation. 5.3 The level of delegation and responsibility of the manager, and the lines of accountability, are clearly defined. 5.4 Clear arrangements are in place to identify the person in charge when the manager is absent.	*This standard increases the level of monitoring required of the fostering service's executive and places a greater individual responsibility upon the service's manager. The standard concludes with specific measures to be taken to address the communication needs of children.* • Increased expectation that *the manager* regularly monitors 'all records' for compliance, analysis and action when required (25.2). In the 2002 standards this expectation tended to be allocated more generally to the *fostering service* (e.g. 2002 9.4 and 13.6) or by reference to *management systems* (e.g. 2002 9.5 and 25.3). • New reference to volunteers (25.4 and 25.9) echoing standard 24 above. • New expectation to make Ofsted reports available to various parties (25.6). • New monitoring expectations made of those responsible for the governance of the service to monitor finances, outcomes and compliance with registration **on a quarterly basis** (25.7). • New expectation that, in the information about the disclosure of foster carer payments to commissioners, a distinction is drawn between fees and allowances (25.10).

2011 standards	Related 2002 standard	What's new? What's changed?
25.7 The executive side of the local authority or the independent foster service's provider/trustees, board members or management committee members: **a** receive written reports on the management, outcomes and financial state of the fostering service every 3 months; **b** monitor the management and outcomes of the services in order to satisfy themselves that the service is effective and is achieving good outcomes for children; **c** satisfy themselves that the provider is complying with the conditions of registration. **25.8** The registered person takes action to address any issues of concern that they identify or which is raised with them. **25.9** Staff, volunteers and foster carers have a copy of: **a** the policies and working practices in respect of grievances and disciplinary matters; **b** details of the services offered; **c** the equal opportunities policy; **d** health and safety procedures. **25.10** Information is provided to commissioners of services as part of tendering. This includes: **a** charges for each of its services; **b** statements of the amounts paid to foster carers (separated by fee and allowance); and **c** any amounts paid for other services, e.g. health and education.	**16.16** Staff have a copy of: ● the policies and working practices in respect of grievances and disciplinary matters ● details of the services offered ● the equal opportunities policy ● health and safety procedures. **22.8** Information about the procedures for dealing with complaints and representations is widely available. Complaints and representations are recorded and monitored and the outcome evaluated to inform future provision of services.	● New expectations regarding responding to communication issues, including those related to disability and when English is not the child's first language (25.12). ● The reference to conflicts of interest in the 2002 standards (2002, 4.5) is not present in the 2011 standards although it is mentioned in the statutory guidance (see paragraphs 4.12 and 5.35).

2011 standards	Related 2002 standard	What's new? What's changed?
25.11 The registered person has provided the service with a written policy and procedural guidelines on considering and responding to representations and complaints in accordance with legal requirements and relevant statutory guidance.		
25.12 The service has the facilities to work with children with physical, sensory and learning impairments, communication difficulties or for whom English is not their first language. Oral and written communications are made available in a format which is appropriate to the physical, sensory and learning impairments, communication difficulties and language of the individual. The procedures include arrangements for reading, translating, Makaton, pictures, tape recording and explaining documents to those people who are unable to understand the document.		

RECORDS

2011 standards	Related 2002 standard	What's new? What's changed?
Standard 26 Records 26.1 The fostering service has and implements a written policy that clarifies the purpose, format and content of information to be kept on the fostering service's files, on the child's files and on case files relating to foster carers. 26.2 Staff, volunteers, panel members and fostering households understand the nature of records maintained and follow the service's policy for the keeping and retention of files, managing confidential information and access to files (including files removed from the premises). There is a system in place to monitor the quality and adequacy of record keeping and take action when needed. 26.3 Children and their parents understand the nature of records maintained and how to access them. 26.4 Information about individual children is kept confidential and only shared with those who have a legitimate and current need to know the information, and to those parts of a child's record or other information that they need to know. 26.5 Entries in records, decisions and reasons, are legible, clearly expressed, non-stigmatising and distinguish between fact, opinion and third party information, and are signed and dated. 26.6 Information about the child is recorded clearly and in a way which will be helpful to the child when they access their files now or in the future. Children are actively encouraged to read their files, other than necessarily confidential or third party information, and to correct errors and add personal statements.	24.1 The fostering service ensures that an up-to-date, comprehensive case record is maintained for each child or young person in foster care which details the nature and quality of care provided and contributes to an understanding of her/his life events. Relevant information from the case records is made available to the child and to anyone involved in her/his care. 24.2 There is a written policy on case recording which establishes the purpose, format and contents of files, and clarifies what information is kept on the foster carer's files and what information is kept on the child's files. 24.3 Where there is an agency placement, the agency works with the responsible authority to ensure effective integration of information held in the agency's case files and those of the responsible authority. The agency provides copies of the records and documents in relation to children placed by a responsible authority immediately, on receipt of a written request. When a child leaves an agency foster care placement, the agency sends all relevant records to the responsible authority. 24.4 The fostering service ensures that the foster carer knows why the child is in foster care and understands the basis for the current placement, its intended duration and purpose, and the details of the child's legal status. 24.5 The foster carer encourages the child to reflect on and understand her/his history, according to the child's age and ability, and to keep appropriate memorabilia. The fostering service makes this role clear to their foster carers.	*This standard sets out the policy and quality assurance expectations in relation to records. The active promotion of records as a tool for enabling a child to understand their past is emphasised in this standard. The transfer of records when foster carers move between services is addressed in this standard.* ● As in standards 24 and 25 above, new reference to volunteers in relation to records (26.2). ● New mention of arrangements for when files are 'removed from the premises' (26.2). ● New focus upon the child accessing their records as an adult, and greater emphasis upon 'actively' encouraging children to read their files (26.6). ● The expectation that foster carers will be provided with *training* regarding how to record significant life events for children (2002, 24.7) is *not* present in the 2011 standards, although there remains a clear expectation that the importance of this work is emphasised to foster carers (26.6). ● New emphasis upon the integration of records held by the independent fostering provider with those held by the commissioning local authority (26.8).

2011 standards	Related 2002 standard	What's new? What's changed?
26.7 The foster carer understands the important supporting role they play in encouraging the child to reflect on and understand their history. The child, subject to age and understanding, is encouraged to keep appropriate memorabilia (including photographs) of their time in the placement. The fostering service makes this role clear to their foster carers and ensures they can record, and help children make a record of (subject to age and understanding), significant life events.	**24.6** The fostering service gives the foster carer access to all relevant information to help the child understand and come to terms with past events. (Where necessary information is not forthcoming from the responsible authority, a copy of the written request for information is kept.).	• New expectation to share foster carer information with a new agency when a foster carer transfers between services **within one month** of receipt of request (26.9). Regulation 26(2)(d) sets out that the approval of the foster carer must have been terminated before the transfer of records. The relevant statutory guidance outlines that assessment interviews – for example, of previous partners – carried out by a previous agency need not be repeated by the receiving agency (see paragraph 5.30 of the statutory guidance).
26.8 Where there is an agency placement, the agency works with the responsible authority to ensure effective integration of information held in the agency's case files and those of the responsible authority. On receipt of a written request by a child's responsible authority, the agency immediately provides copies of records and documents in relation to the child.	**24.7** The carer is trained and provided with the necessary equipment to record significant life events for the child, and to encourage the child to make such recordings, including photograph albums.	
26.9 When a foster carer seeks to move to a new provider, the new provider seeks information from the previous provider about the prospective foster carer, and the previous provider complies with such a request within one month of receipt of the written request.	**24.8** The fostering service ensures that their carers store information in a secure manner and understand what information they are expected to keep and what information needs to be passed on to the fostering service.	
	25.1 The fostering service's administrative records contain all significant information relevant to the running of the foster care service and as required by regulations.	
	25.2 Separate records are kept for: • staff, employed and independent/sessional carers; • children; • complaints; • allegations.	
	25.3 There is a system to monitor the quality and adequacy of records, and remedial action is taken when necessary.	
	25.4 Confidential records are stored securely at all times and there is a clear policy on access.	

2011 standards	Related 2002 standard	What's new? What's changed?
	25.5 Records are in a form which can be readily passed on if a child moves to another placement, or ceases to be looked after or if references are requested on a member of staff or carer.	
	25.6 There is a permanent, private, secure record for each child and foster carer referred to or appointed by the organisation. This can, in compliance with legal requirements for safeguards, be seen by the child and by her/his parents or foster carers.	
	25.7 There is a written policy and procedural guidance for staff for the keeping and retention of case files ensuring that foster carers, fostered children and their parents know the nature of the records maintained and how to access them.	
	25.8 There is a procedure on storing and managing confidential information that is known to panel members, staff and specialist advisers.	
	25.9 Written entries in records are legible, clearly expressed, non-stigmatising, and distinguish between fact, opinion and third party information.	
	25.10 The system for keeping records is congruent with the Looking After Children System/Integrated Children's System.	
	25.11 Records are kept of checks and references that have been obtained and their outcomes.	
	25.12 Children and foster carers are encouraged to access their records, make additions and comments and record personal statements, including any dissent.	

PREMISES

2011 standards	Related 2002 standard	What's new? What's changed?
Standard 27 Fitness of premises for use as fostering service	26.1 Premises used as offices by the fostering service are appropriate for the purpose.	*This standard addresses the increasingly common requirement across all sectors to carry out contingency planning.*
27.1 There are efficient and robust administrative systems, including IT and communication systems. Premises have:	26.2 There are identifiable office premises to which staff and others with a legitimate interest have access during normal office hours.	• New expectation to have a Business Continuity Plan (27.3).
a facilities for the secure retention of records;	26.3 There are efficient and robust administrative systems, including IT and communication systems. Premises have:	
b appropriate measures to safeguard IT systems; and	• facilities for the secure retention of records in a lockable room;	
c an appropriate security system.	• appropriate measures to safeguard IT systems; and	
27.2 The premises and its contents are insured (or there are alternative prompt methods of replacing lost items).	• an appropriate security system.	
27.3 The provider has a Business Continuity Plan, which staff understand and can access, which will include both provision of premises and safeguarding/back up of records.	26.4 Premises provide an equipped base from which staff work.	
	26.5 The premises and its contents are adequately insured (or there are alternative prompt methods of replacing lost items).	

PAYMENT TO CARERS

2011 standards	Related 2002 standard	What's new? What's changed?

Standard 28 Payment to carers

28.1 Each foster carer receives at least the national minimum allowance for the child, plus any necessary agreed expenses for the care, education and reasonable leisure interests of the child, including insurance, holidays, birthdays, school trips, religious festivals etc, which cover the full cost of caring for each child placed with her/him.

28.2 Payments of allowances and any fees paid are made promptly at the agreed time and foster carers are provided with a statement of payment at the end of each tax year.

28.3 Allowances and any fees paid are reviewed annually and the fostering service consults with foster carers in advance of any change to the allowance and fee.

28.4 The fostering service advises foster carers of financial and other support that is available to foster carers where a child remains with them after they reach the age of 18 or where they care for/provide a home for a child and their parent(s).

28.5 There is a clear and transparent written policy on payments to foster carers that sets out the criteria for calculating payments and distinguishes between the allowance paid and any fee paid. The policy includes policy on payment of allowances and any fee during a break in placement or should the fostering household be subject to an allegation.

29.1 Each foster carer receives an allowance and agreed expenses, which cover the full cost of caring for each child or young person placed with him or her. Payments are made promptly and at the agreed time. Allowances and fees are reviewed annually.

29.2 There is a written policy on fostering allowances. This and the current allowance levels are well publicised and provided annually to each carer. The carer receives clear information about the allowances and expenses payable and how to access them, before a child is placed.

This standard sets out greater levels of consistency and transparency in the payment of foster carers.

- New expectation to pay the government-set national minimum allowance and to meet 'full costs' related to other child-related expenses (28.1).

- New expectation to provide annual statement at the end of each tax year (28.2).

- New expectation to advise foster carers of the support available once a foster child has reached 18 (28.4).

- New specific reference to clarity in relation to the financial support of parent and child placements (28.4).

- New emphasis upon transparency and clarity of payment (28.5).

- New expectation that payment during breaks from fostering and during investigations into allegations are *clarified* in the written policy (28.5) although it falls short of *requiring* any such payments. See also standard 22.11.

- New expectation of equality of approach to payment systems, regardless of anticipated duration of the placement (long-term or short-term) or whether the foster child is related to the carer (28.7). See also standard 30.10.

- New clarity demanded regarding the status of equipment made available to foster carers (28.8).

- New specific emphasis upon ensuring disabled children access the benefits they are entitled to and that they are spent appropriately (28.9).

2011 standards	Related 2002 standard	What's new? What's changed?
28.6 The written policy and the current level of payments are provided annually to each foster carer and commissioners of the service. The foster carer receives clear information about the allowances and expenses payable, and how to access them, before a child is placed.		
28.7 Criteria for calculating fees and allowances are applied equally to all foster carers, whether the foster carer is related to the child or unrelated, or the placement is short- or long-term.		
28.8 Fostering service providers are clear about what equipment is being either loaned or given to foster carers.		
28.9 Where a child is eligible for benefits as a result of a disability, foster carers are encouraged to apply for those benefits. There are regular recorded discussions about how any additional benefits are being spent to promote the best interests of the child.		

NOTIFICATIONS

2011 standards	Related 2002 standard	What's new? What's changed?
Standard 29 Notification of significant events 29.1 The registered person has a system in place to notify, within 24 hours, persons and appropriate authorities of the occurrence of significant events in accordance with regulation 36. The system includes what to do where a notifiable event arises at the weekend. 29.2 A written record is kept which includes details of the action taken, and the outcome of any action or investigation, following a notifiable event. 29.3 The registered person has a system for notification to responsible authorities of any serious concerns about the emotional or mental health of a child, such that a mental health assessment would be requested under the Mental Health Act 1983. 29.4 Following an incident notifiable under regulation 36, the registered person contacts the responsible authority to discuss any further action that may need to be taken.	Note: Notifications were addressed in the Fostering Services Regulations (2002) in the Schedules 7 and 8 but not cited in the 2002 standards themselves.	*Although the notification requirements in the regulations are largely unchanged, this standard places a new emphasis upon responding to mental health issues for foster children.* ● New reference to the arrangements for responding to notifiable events at the weekend (29.1). ● New emphasis upon mental health issues of the foster child, not specifically addressed in the current regulations (29.3).

FAMILY AND FRIENDS CARERS

2011 standards	Related 2002 standard	What's new? What's changed?
Standard 30 Family and friends as foster carers	**32.1** These standards are all relevant to carers who are family and friends of the child, but there is a recognition of the particular relationship and position of family and friends carers.	*Much of this standard is new, reflecting the research and practice development in this area of fostering since 2002 and taking account of the newly issued statutory guidance. There is an interesting caveat regarding independent fostering providers at the end of the standard.*
30.1 The needs and circumstances of family and friends foster carers are taken into account when determining the fostering service's policies and practices.		
30.2 The fostering service's Statement of Purpose includes the services and facilities that they provide to family and friends foster carers.	**32.2** Local authority fostering services are sensitive to pre-existing relationships in assessing and approving family and friends as foster carers.	• New expectation that family and friends carers are integrated in the service's policies and practices (30.1).
30.3 In deciding whether a relative, friend or other connected person should be approved as a foster carer, the decision maker takes into account the needs, wishes and feelings of the child and the capacity of the carer to meet these.	**32.3** The support and training needs for family and friends carers are assessed and met in the same way as for any other carers.	• New expectation to address family and friends in Statement of Purpose (30.2). • Criteria to be used by agency decision-maker when considering approval of a friends and family foster carer established as the carer's capacity to meet the needs of the child (30.3). Similar criteria are to be applied for assessments, with an emphasis upon the child's wishes and feelings (30.5).
30.4 In seeking to support family and friends foster carers, the local authority fostering service works closely with the wider local authority children's services department, other departments, and agencies such as housing, to mitigate any limitations to the carer's capacity to care for a foster child.	**32.4** The mechanisms within a local authority fostering service for assessing and approving family and friends carers are designed in a way that encourages their consideration as carers.	• New expectation to work with other local authority departments, with the example of housing offered (30.4).
30.5 When assessing an individual's suitability to be a family and friends foster carer, the likely length of the placement, the age of the child, the wishes and feelings and any concerns of the child and, if appropriate, the capacity of the wider family to contribute to the child's long term care, are taken into account.		• Emphasis upon the need for clarity in the assessment process reflecting concerns identified in research that prospective family and friends foster carers have not always had the purpose and process of the assessment explained to them with sufficient clarity (30.6).

2011 standards	Related 2002 standard	What's new? What's changed?
30.6 Potential family and friends foster carers should be provided with information about the assessment process, so they know what is expected of them, how they will be assessed, including the criteria that will be used and how particular issues for family and friends foster carers will be addressed, and any support offered during the assessment process. **30.7** Family and friends foster carers are asked about their existing knowledge of the foster child's behaviour and background and any concerns they have about the child, as well being provided with information about the child that is held by the fostering service. **30.8** The child's introduction to the new fostering arrangement takes account of the fact that, whilst the child may know the carer well, the carer's role in the child's life is now changing. This is explained to the child and the carer is provided with the support they need to manage this transition. **30.9** The fostering service takes into account the carer's, parents' and child's views about contact before the start of the placement, or as soon as possible afterwards, and puts in place appropriate supports to help manage contact. **30.10** Financial and other support is provided to all foster carers according to objective criteria that do not discriminate against foster carers who have a pre-existing relationship with the child. Family and friends foster carers may require some services to be delivered in a different way, but there should be equity of provision and entitlement.		• Emphasis upon asking prospective friends and family foster carers about *their* knowledge of the child, as well providing full information *to* them (30.7). • Emphasis upon the need to clearly explain the implications of taking on a formal foster carer role to prospective friends and family foster carers and the child (30.8). • Expectation to consult specifically, and plan appropriately, regarding proposed contact arrangements (30.9). • Echoing standard 28.7 related to payments, specific prohibition against any support that discriminates against family and friends carers (30.10). • New emphasis upon equality of access to training, including bespoke training and support (30.12 and 30.13). • Requirement to work within the timescales set out in the Care Planning Regulations 2010 (30.14). • The caveat in bold at the end of the standard, although addressing the fact that this standard is not generally relevant for most independent fostering providers, does allow for agencies other than local authorities to carry out this type of approval.

2011 standards	Related 2002 standard	What's new? What's changed?
30.11 Family and friends foster carers have access to training available to other foster carers, but the fostering service provider also offers training that addresses the particular needs and circumstances of family and friends foster carers.		
30.12 Family and friends foster carers have access to support groups that meet their particular needs.		
30.13 Supervising social workers who are supporting family and friends foster carers have training in the particular needs and circumstances of this group.		
30.14 Where a family and friends foster carer is temporarily approved as a foster carer under regulation 24 of the Care Planning, Placement and Case Review (England) Regulations 2010, a full assessment is competed as soon as practicable, where the intention is for the child to stay with the carer, and always within the statutory timeframe set out in the regulations.		
This standard only applies to local authority fostering services and those independent fostering services which approve family and friends foster carers. However, when family and friends are approved as foster carers the other standards apply as they do for other foster carers.		

PLACEMENT PLAN AND REVIEW

2011 standards	Related 2002 standard	What's new? What's changed?
Standard 31 Placement Plan and review 31.1 The fostering service supports foster carers to play an active role in agreeing the contents of each child's placement plan, in conjunction with the responsible authority. 31.2 The foster carer is given a copy of the child's placement plan as soon as this is provided to them by the responsible authority. If provision of the care plan by the responsible authority is delayed, the fostering service provider follows this up with the responsible authority. 31.3 The foster carer is supported to contribute effectively to the review of their care plan, which includes the placement plan. 31.4 The foster carer is supported to assist the child to put forward their views, wishes and feelings as part of each review process, and the fostering service helps to ensure that these are fully taken into account by the child's responsible authority. 31.5 The fostering service supports foster carers to explain the child's care plan and any changes to those plans, to the child.	Note: This standard addresses areas largely covered by Schedule 6 of Fostering Services Regulations 2002 but not covered directly by the 2002 standards. The need for child-specific information is cited in the 2002 standards (e.g. 2002, 10.2, 12.8 and 13.3) but not gathered into a single standard area.	***Nearly all of this standard is new, partly because it relates to the Care Planning Regulations 2010. The key message of the standards is that the foster carer and the foster child both need to understand and contribute towards the Placement Plan, which is seen as the most important document for achieving clarity of purpose for all parties.*** ● New emphasis upon the 'active' role to be taken by foster carers in relation to the Placement Plan (31.1 and 31.3). ● 31.2 contains a minor drafting error: 'them' in the first sentence should probably refer to the 'fostering service'. ● Clear expectation that the placement plan is provided to the foster carer. ● Emphasis upon the foster carer assisting the child in the expression of their views as part of the review process (31.4) and understanding the care plan (31.5), echoing the reference to an advocacy role for foster carers in relation to a child's education (8.4, 8.5 and 8.7). ● Expectation that the fostering service will actively pursue regulatory compliance in terms of frequency of reviews with the responsible authority (31.6). ● Mirroring the first standard (1.5), the final standard emphasises the child's right to independent advocacy, this time in relation to statutory reviews (31.8).

2011 standards	Related 2002 standard	What's new? What's changed?
31.6 The fostering service contacts the responsible authority to request statutory reviews or visits if these are overdue for any child, or if a review has not already been arranged by the responsible authority and a change in the care plan is needed, there has been a significant change in arrangements for the child's care or a major action (e.g. a change of placement) which is not in the care plan appears likely.		
31.7 The fostering service and foster carer contribute effectively to each child's Placement Plan review and statutory review of the child's care plan.		
31.8 Children are assisted to secure an independent advocate to support them in providing their views, wishes and feelings to statutory reviews.		

Part 2: The regulations

Note: throughout the Fostering Services (England) Regulations 2011, the term 'Chief Inspector' replaces the term 'Commission' used in the Fostering Services Regulations 2002 in light of the change of inspectorate.

Topic area	2011 regulation	Equivalent 2002 regulation	What's new? What's changed?
Citation, commencement and extent	1	1	No significant changes
Interpretation	2	2	New and updated definitions to address the requirements of the Care Planning Regulations 2010, e.g. references to the 'independent reviewing officer' and the 'placement plan'.
Statement of purpose and children's guide	3	3	No significant changes
Review of statement of purpose and children's guide	4	4	No significant changes
Fitness of provider	5	5	No significant changes
Appointment of manager	6	6	No significant changes
Fitness of manager	7	7	No significant changes
Registered person – general requirements	8	8	No significant changes
Notification of offences	9	9	No significant changes
Local authority service – manager	10	10	No significant changes
Independent fostering agencies – duty to secure welfare	11	11	No significant changes

Topic area	2011 regulation	Equivalent 2002 regulation	What's new? What's changed?
Arrangements for the protection of children	12	12	New requirement for the safeguarding policy to include reference to parent and child placements as follows: *Regulation 12(2): The written policy must include a statement of measures to be taken to safeguard any child before making parent and child arrangements with that foster parent.* See also Statutory Guidance paragraph 3.67.
Behaviour management and children missing from foster parent's home	13	13	No changes aside from change of the term from 'absence from the foster parent's home' to 'children missing', reflecting the national policy initiatives since the drafting of the 2002 regulations.
Duty to promote contact	14	14	Reference to 'care plan' rather than 'foster placement agreement' to take account of the term used in the Care Planning Regulations 2010.
Health of children placed with foster parents	15	15	No significant changes, aside from clarification of the meaning of the term 'general medical practitioner' to ensure they are registered with the General Medical Council.
Education, employment and leisure activities	16	16	No significant changes
Support, training and information for foster parents	17	17	Reference to the 'most recent version of the child's care plan' as the means of conveying information about the foster child to the foster carer, taking account of the requirements of the Care Planning Regulations 2010.
Independent fostering agencies – complaints and representations	18	18	No significant changes
Staffing of the fostering service	19	19	No significant changes

Topic area	2011 regulation	Equivalent 2002 regulation	What's new? What's changed?
Fitness of workers	20	20	A significant change is achieved by omission in this regulation. The prohibition upon employing a foster carer or a member of the foster carer's household in the 2002 regulations (2002 regulations 20(6) and 20(7)) has now gone. The implications are twofold. See paragraphs 4.12 of the statutory guidance regarding employing foster carers and paragraph 5.35 of the statutory guidance regarding the recruitment of employees as foster carers.
Employment of staff	21	21	No significant changes
Records with respect to fostering agencies	22	22	The 2011 regulations combine the 2002 regulations 22 and 23 so that the fitness of premises (2002 regulation 23) is covered under the heading of records. The 2002 regulation 23 regarding 'Fitness of premises' has been deleted, although the 2011 statutory guidance does set out expectations in relation to secure storage of paper and electronic records (paragraph 5.78).
Constitution and membership of the fostering panel (described as 'Establishment of the fostering panel' in the 2002 regulations)	23	24	There are some significant changes to the membership requirements of fostering panels, including the following: ● the establishment of a 'central list'; ● the requirement to have an independent chair; ● the potential to have two vice chairs (who need not be independent); ● the requirement to have a social worker member with three years' post-qualification experience. This member need not be employed by the fostering service.

Topic area	2011 regulation	Equivalent 2002 regulation	What's new? What's changed?
Meetings of fostering panel	24	25	The quorum for panel meetings has been significantly altered by this regulation. The number of panel members required remains five, consisting of the following: ● a chair or a vice chair; ● a social worker member; ● a member providing independence if the chair is absent and the vice chair is not independent.
Functions of the fostering panel	25	26	There is a new emphasis upon the panel considering all the information provided to it, as well as ensuring it has appropriate information and advice before reaching a recommendation. The emphasis upon seeking any legal or medical advice it 'considers necessary' is also new in this context.
Assessment of prospective foster parents	26	27	Although much of this regulation is the same, there is new provision regarding the transfer, with the foster carer's consent, of information between agencies when a foster carer wishes to move between fostering services once the approval has been terminated (including when they have resigned). Regulation 26 (2)(d) sets this out below: *(d) where X was approved as a foster parent by another fostering service provider and that approval has been terminated, and where X consents to the inspection, the fostering service provider may request inspection of the relevant records compiled by that other fostering service provider in relation to X under regulations 30 and 31.* There are some adjustments to the specified offences set out in the regulations, including a new reference to Sexual Offences Act 2003. See also the new Schedule 4.

Topic area	2011 regulation	Equivalent 2002 regulation	What's new? What's changed?
Approval of foster parents	27	28	The 2011 regulations absorb and consolidate the Fostering Services (Amendment) Regulations 2009 in relation to the right to appeal either to the local authority or to the Independent Review Mechanism in response to a 'qualifying determination' (Independent Review of Determinations (Adoption and Fostering) Regulations 2009). Another aspect of the 2009 amendments, in relation to panel member tenure, is not consolidated in the 2011 regulations: the 2011 regulations do not place any limit on the tenure of panel members. See paragraph 5.13 of the statutory guidance.
Reviews and terminations of approval	28	29a (as described in the 2009 amendment to the 2002 regulations)	
Information to be sent to independent review panel	29		
Case records relating to foster parents and others	30	30	There is an important amendment to take account of the new expectations regarding the assessment of 'connected people' (friends and family carers) under the Care Planning Regulations 2010. This now refers to regulation 24 of the Care Planning Regulations 2010, rather than the 2002 reference to regulation 38 of the Fostering Services Regulations 2002.
Register of foster parents	31	31	As above, references to regulation 38 of the 2002 Fostering Services Regulations are replaced by references to regulation 24 of the Care Planning Regulations 2010.
Retention and confidentiality of records	32	32	There is a new additional provision to require the transfer of foster carer records within one month of receipt of the request, as set out below: *32(6) A fostering service provider must make their records compiled under regulation 30 or 31 in relation to a foster parent available for inspection by another fostering service provider within one month of a request under regulation 26(2)(d).*

Topic area	2011 regulation	Equivalent 2002 regulation	What's new? What's changed?
Placements	No equivalent regulations	33 to 41	The requirements regarding the planning and reviewing of placements set out in The Fostering Services Regulations 2002 regulations 33 to 41 are now addressed in the Care Planning Regulations 2010 and are no longer covered here.
Fostering agency ceasing to carry out fostering functions – notifications and records	33	No equivalent regulation	Regulations 33 and 34 seek to minimise the impact upon children and foster carers in the event of any closure of a fostering service. 33(3) is significant because, for the first time in this regulatory context, it sets out how, in the absence of a transfer to any other fostering service or local authority, the local authority where the closing service is situated 'by default will take over responsibility for the agency's approved carers' (statutory guidance paragraph 5.74).
Fostering agency ceasing to carry out fostering functions – new fostering service providers	34	No equivalent regulation	Following the yardstick set out for 'connected people' in the Care Planning Regulations 2010, this regulation outlines a time frame of 16 weeks within which the receiving agency should aim to assess a foster carer transferring from a closing agency.
Review of quality of care	35	42	No significant changes
Notifiable events	36	43	No significant changes
Financial position	37	44	No significant changes
Notice of absence	38	45	No significant changes
Notice of changes	39	46	No significant changes
Appointment of liquidators, etc	40	47	No significant changes .
Offences	No equivalent regulation	48	The 2002 regulation 48 concerning offences is deleted.
Compliance with regulations	41	49	No significant changes

Topic area	2011 regulation	Equivalent 2002 regulation	What's new? What's changed?
Application of these regulations with modifications to short breaks	42	No equivalent regulation	This is an important amendment, setting out the exemptions for short breaks related to contact, health and education. Perhaps surprisingly, the regulatory exemptions are not consistent with those in the standards, which relate to identity and diversity, contact and promoting independence. The new thresholds set out in the Care Planning Regulations 2010 (17 days for a single episode; 75 days per year in total) for regarding episodes of short break care as a single placement are followed here.
Amendment of regulations	43	Not applicable	This is tidying up the references to the 2002 regulations in the 2010 Care Planning Regulations.
Revocation of regulations	44	Not applicable	A regulation confirming the revocation of the Fostering Services Regulations 2002.
Transitional provisions	45	Not applicable	These set out the transitional arrangements in place until 30.9.11. See also paragraph 5.10 of the statutory guidance.
Information required in respect of persons seeking to carry on, manage or work for the purposes of a fostering service	Schedule 1	Schedule 1	No significant changes
Records to be kept by fostering service providers	Schedule 2	Schedule 2	No significant changes
Information as to prospective foster parent ("X") and other members of their household and family	Schedule 3	Schedule 3	No significant changes
Offences specified for the purposes of regulation 26(7)(b)	Schedule 4	Schedule 4	New references to specified offences in England related to regulation 26.

Topic area	2011 regulation	Equivalent 2002 regulation	What's new? What's changed?
Matters and obligations in foster carer agreements	Schedule 5	Schedule 5	The 'Placement Plan' from the Care Planning Regulations 2010 replaces the term 'foster placement agreement'. (See Statutory Guidance Volume 2, 'Care Planning, Placement and Case Review', paragraph 3.129.) There is no longer a reference to allowing the removal of a child: this is because the ending of placement is covered by the Care Planning Regulations 2010, not these regulations. Similarly, the 2002 Schedule 6 is not present in the 2011 version. The 2002 Schedule 6 concerned 'Foster Placement Agreements'. All the requirements related to the Placement Plan can now be found in the Care Planning Regulations 2010.
Matters to be monitored by the registered person	Schedule 6	Schedule 7	No significant changes, aside from removal of the reference to 'duty rosters', which has been accepted as based upon children's homes and consequently deleted.
Events and notifications	Schedule 7	Schedule 8	No significant changes. There is one change to the notification table, outlining how the area authority must be informed of the 'instigation and outcome of any child protection enquiry involving a child placed with foster parents', but this is already covered by the expectations of *Working Together to Safeguard Children* (DCSF, 2010).

CHAPTER 3
Are you ready?
An action planning format

Introduction

Given that the 2011 standards, regulations and guidance consolidate a number of policy and practice initiatives over recent years, many of the "new" elements may well have already been actioned by fostering services. Other elements, though, may be less familiar. Some of the new expectations are located across different parts of the new documents, making action planning potentially difficult. The following format aims to save time for fostering services by drawing together the new expectations from different places across the guidance, regulations and standards in a way that assists self-audit and action planning.

This action planning tool makes no claim to be exhaustive. For example, the introduction of the concept of resilience in the standards and guidance, while undoubtedly important, requires considered planning in terms of the induction, training and supervision of staff and foster carers rather than specific and immediate action. These more subtle changes of emphasis in the standards, regulation and statutory guidance are not addressed here. For the detail of the new expectations and requirements, managers and practitioners are referred to the tables in Chapter 2.

Instead, this format aims to draw together some of the new expectations in the following four broad areas of practice.

- What's new in terms of the fostering panel and agency decision making?
- What's new in terms of policy expectations?
- What's new in terms of training?
- What's new in terms of management oversight?

Explanatory note

In the following format, the term 'SG' (Statutory Guidance) is used to refer to the new *Children Act Guidance Volume 4: Fostering Services*, followed by the relevant paragraph number. The term 'Standard' refers to the Fostering Services: National Minimum Standards 2011, and unless otherwise specified, the term 'Regulation' refers to The Fostering Services (England) Regulations 2011.

The right hand column – 'Are you ready? What, if anything, needs to change?' – is left blank for notes and commentary to assist in self-audit.

ARE YOU READY? A SELF-AUDIT AND ACTION PLANNING TEMPLATE

1 What's new in terms of the fostering panel and agency decision making?

New expectations related to the fostering panel and the decision making process can be found across the statutory guidance, standards and regulations. The following draws these together.

New expectation	Where is the basis of the new expectation?	Commentary	Are you ready? What, if anything, needs to change?
Composition	Regulation 23(1) Standard 14.1 and 14.8 SG 5.4 to 5.8	Fostering services will need to consider who, and how many, they want on their 'central list'. A balance needs to be struck between developing a breadth of experience and expertise while remaining mindful of retaining a 'core membership' (SG 5.4) to ensure coherence. One potentially useful approach would be to determine initially the 'core membership' and then develop a longer 'central list' over time, in part as a contingency measure to avoid any problems achieving a quorum; in part as a way of broadening the specialisms and knowledge base that panel meetings can then draw upon as needed.	
Induction of those on the central list	Standard 23.9	There is an expectation that the induction of those on the central list will be completed within ten weeks of joining the list, not within ten weeks of attending a panel meeting.	
Opportunity to observe the panel for those on the central list	Standard 23.8	It is expected that anyone on the central list is offered the opportunity to observe panel prior to joining.	

New expectation	Where is the basis of the new expectation?	Commentary	Are you ready? What, if anything, needs to change?
Training of all those on the central list	Standard 23.10 and 23.11	The expectation that all those on the central list are given the opportunity to attend an annually held joint panel and service training day (23.10), and 'kept abreast of relevant changes to legislation and guidance' (23.11) through training and skills development implies that the decision to include someone on the central list should not be taken too lightly. So although there is no formal limit placed on the size on the central list, fostering services will inevitably need to remain mindful of these resource and logistical implications.	
Quorum checklist	Regulation 24(1) SG 5.19	Although the panel quorum is more relaxed than before, a simple checklist ensuring the three requirements are fulfilled (chair/vice chair, the social worker and an element of independence within the five members present) may be useful to ensure consistent compliance. Note that the required social work member can now also be independent.	
Appointment of independent chair	Regulation 23(4)(i) SG 5.9 to 5.11	The transitional arrangements that apply up to 30.9.11 are set out in regulation 45 and SG 5.10. The definition of independence used in this context, as defined in SG 5.9, enables a local authority to appoint someone also employed by the same local authority but not directly involved in fostering (with the example provided of someone employed by the education service).	

New expectation	Where is the basis of the new expectation?	Commentary	Are you ready? What, if anything, needs to change?
Consideration of two vice chairs	Regulation 23(4)(ii) SG 5.12	Although it is described as 'preferable' in the guidance for vice chairs to be independent, this is not a requirement. There is also no requirement to have two vice chairs.	
Annual appraisal of panel members against agreed performance objectives	SG 5.15	The statutory guidance outlines that the chair should conduct the annual appraisal of the other panel members.	
Annual appraisal of the independent chair against agreed performance objectives	SG 5.15	The statutory guidance outlines that the annual appraisal of the independent chair should be carried out by the agency decision maker, and based upon feedback from presenting social workers, prospective foster carers attending panel and other panel members. The appraisal may also be based upon the agency decision maker's observation of the chair at panel meetings. This is a suggestion in the guidance, not a requirement.	
Named medical and legal advisers to the panel	Standard 14.6 SG 5.24	The statutory guidance suggests that this is 'best provided by the identification of a named medical adviser and legal adviser to the panel' (SG 5.24). The advisers do not need to be panel members. In practice, medical advice will generally already be provided to panels because of considerations relating to approval and reviews. The provision of a named legal adviser, though, may require further consideration.	

New expectation	Where is the basis of the new expectation?	Commentary	Are you ready? What, if anything, needs to change?
Minutes used as the basis of decision making	Regulation 24(2) Standard 14.7 and 14.9 SG 5.23 and SG 5.25	The agency decision needs to be taken within seven working days of receiving a 'final set of panel minutes' (standard 14.9). The minutes need to be 'full and accurate' (SG 5.25). Although standard 14.7 implies that the chair has a lead function in ensuring the minutes' accuracy, the Re B case (see Adoption Statutory Guidance Chapter 2 paragraph 64 (4)) ruled that minutes should be agreed by all those who attended panel *prior* to decision making. In order to comply with the expectation that decisions are only based upon 'final' minutes, services may wish to consider seeking any amendments from panel members and those attending panel in the days following the panel meeting rather than, as is usually the case currently, awaiting the next panel meeting.	
Timescales for paperwork to panel members	Standard 14.3	All papers need to be circulated at least five working days prior to the panel meeting.	

New expectation	Where is the basis of the new expectation?	Commentary	Are you ready? What, if anything, needs to change?
Social work qualification of agency decision maker	Standard 23.12 SG 5.39	The decision maker is expected to be a social worker with three years' post-qualification experience and knowledge of childcare law and practice. The statutory guidance permits the appointment of more than one decision maker, but the requirement to be a social worker applies to all those carrying out decision making functions. This may have implications for some services: a peer head of service, for example, from a non-social work discipline could not "step in" for the usual decision maker.	
Heightened expectations regarding the decision making process	Standard 14.9 SG 5.40 and 5.41	The bullet points set out for decision making in paragraph 5.40 of the statutory guidance can be readily turned into a decision making template. Such a template may prove particularly useful for more contentious or finely balanced decisions.	
Timescales related to decision making	Standard 14.10	The agency decision must be conveyed orally within two working days of being made and sent in writing within five working days.	
Extension of the quality assurance function of the panel	Standard 14.2 SG 5.10	The rationale for requiring an independent chair given in the statutory guidance is to ensure robust quality assurance. The quality assurance role stated in the 2002 standards related to assessments is now extended to all papers considered by the panel, with potential implications for the systems currently in place to gather feedback from panel members.	

New expectation	Where is the basis of the new expectation?	Commentary	Are you ready? What, if anything, needs to change?
Extension of the quality assurance function of the panel	Standard 14.2 SG 5.10	The rationale for requiring an independent chair given in the statutory guidance is to ensure robust quality assurance. The quality assurance role stated in the 2002 standards related to assessments is now extended to all papers considered by the panel, with potential implications for the systems currently in place to gather feedback from panel members.	
Application to recommendation timescale of eight months	Standard 14.4	Fostering services will want to develop or refine management information systems to take account of the eight month timescale. Panel may wish to be involved in this ongoing monitoring, given that the timing of the recommendation is set as one of the key milestones.	

2   What's new in terms of policy expectations?

Each fostering service policy may well warrant fresh consideration and revision in light of the new expectations to ensure compliance. The following summarises only the explicit references to policies and procedures in the standards, guidance and regulations. Throughout the standards and guidance there are expectations to ensure the policies are known and used by staff, foster carers and children.

New expectation	Where is the basis of the new expectation?	Commentary	Are you ready? What, if anything, needs to change?
Safeguarding policy to address the following: **a) parent and child placements** **b) allegations** **c) clarification about the fees and allowances to be paid during investigation** **d) how to access LSCB procedures and e-safety advice**	Regulation 12 a) Regulation 12(2) Annex B paragraph 12 b) SG 3.67 c) Standard 22.11 Standard 28.5 SG 3.74 d) SG 3.75	There are newly specified areas to be covered in the safeguarding policy, and an expectation that it is made known to children, as well as foster carers and volunteers (standard 22.2). This may require some further thought. Expressing some of the more complex areas of allegation management, for example, in a way that will be useful for children is challenging. Services may wish to consider age-appropriate summaries of the key points for children, as well as user friendly guides for foster carers.	
Complaints and representations policy	Regulation 18 and Schedule 5 and 6 Standard 25.11 SG 3.42 SG 5.50	There is an expectation that local authorities have a complaints procedure that covers issues related to exemptions (SG 5.50), an expectation which may require some consideration for local authorities.	
Administration of medication, treatment and first aid	Standard 6.10 SG 3.60 SG 3.62	The administration of medication policies may require some amendment to take account of the potential for self-administration set out in standard 6.10 and discussed further in the statutory guidance.	
Termination of approval policy	Standard 22.8 SG 3.74	This is a separate policy expectation, distinct from the allegation management policy. This policy requirement may be new for some services.	

New expectation	Where is the basis of the new expectation?	Commentary	Are you ready? What, if anything, needs to change?
Health and safety policy	Standard 10.4 SG 3.82	There are new expectations in the standard for this policy to be regularly reviewed, implying that this policy may require more regular revision than others because of the amount of guidance issued in this area of practice.	
Going missing	Standard 5.2 and 5.4 SG 3.88 to 3.94	There is an emphasis in standard 5.2 upon the foster carers 'knowing' and implementing the policy.	
Acceptable measures of control, restraint and discipline	Regulation 13 Standard 3.8 SG 3.97 to 3.99	Although not new, the statutory guidance again emphasises the need for all foster carers to be aware of this policy, and outlines the areas to be covered in greater detail than previously.	
Staying Put policy	Standard 12.4 and 28.4 SG 3.125	This is a new and challenging policy expectation, outlining that services need to be explicit about how a foster child's transition into adulthood is to be supported and financed.	
Education policies	Standard 8.5 SG 3.103	The emphasis upon foster carers advocating for children to receive a good quality education is based upon a clear policy that they understand.	
Payment to foster carers	Standard 28.5 SG 3.111	There are specific references in the statutory guidance to clarifying exactly what the fostering allowance covers, and which activities or equipment warrant additional payment.	

New expectation	Where is the basis of the new expectation?	Commentary	Are you ready? What, if anything, needs to change?
Recording	Regulation 22 Regulation 26(2)(d) Regulation 32(6) Standard 26 SG 5.75 to 5.79	The retention expectations are set out in the statutory guidance. There are new expectations in terms of the integration of case records between the commissioning authority and the provider, and a focus upon the transfer of records if a foster carer moves between services.	
Disciplinary procedures	SG 4.14	All services should already have a disciplinary procedure for staff. The statutory guidance sets out specific procedural expectations in relation to child protection and the referring on of child protection concerns. This expectation, if not already covered, could potentially be addressed by cross-referencing the disciplinary procedure to the safeguarding policy.	
Whistle blowing	Standard 19.6	The policy expectation itself is not new but, as with other policies, there is a greater emphasis upon ensuring it is known to 'staff, volunteers, foster carers and panel members', perhaps a slightly wider audience than is the case currently in some services.	
Introducing children to placements	Standard 11.1 SG 3.5	Standard 11 sets out a range of new expectations and aspirations that should be incorporated into revised policy statements.	
Fostering panel	Regulation 24 and 25 Standard 14.1	The new expectations related to the fostering panel will require substantial redrafting of the relevant policy documents.	

New expectation	Where is the basis of the new expectation?	Commentary	Are you ready? What, if anything, needs to change?
Parent and child placements	Annex B of the statutory guidance Regulation 12 Standard 28.4	Annex B to the statutory guidance clarifies the regulatory status of parent and child placements, without providing any detailed guidance upon which to base the required policy. Further best practice guidance is anticipated from within the fostering sector.	
Bedroom sharing for those over three	Standard 10.6	Alongside this new expectation in terms of physical space, there is greater prescription about the risk assessment components when contemplating room sharing.	
Back-up carers and overnight stays	Standard 7.3 and 7.7 SG 3.17 to 3.24	The statutory guidance (SG 3.19) conflates two issues: ● overnight stays of children with their friends (i.e. related primarily to the friendships of the child); ● overnight stays of children with relatives of the foster carers (i.e. potentially related primarily to providing a break to the carer in as 'natural' a way as possible). Fostering services will need to develop a policy position consistent with the guidance and standards on both these issues. There are, for example, significant implications in terms of the assessment processes for 'back-up' carers.	

3   What's new in terms of training?

Although reference is made to a core training programme in the statutory guidance (SG 3.58), there is no description of what such a programme should contain. The following seeks to piece together the references to training across the new standards, regulations and guidance.

New expectation	Where is the basis of the new expectation?	Commentary	Are you ready? What, if anything, needs to change?
Health issues and medication	Standard 6.7 and 6.10 SG 3.58	Foster carers should be trained to a level where they are able to: • administer basic first aid and minor illness treatment; • provide advice and support; • meet specific needs arising from a disability, chronic condition or complex needs.	
Risk assessment for foster carers	SG 3.64	Linked with the recurring theme of proportionate risk assessment in the standards and guidance, foster carers are now expected to be trained in risk assessment.	
Health and safety	Standard 10.3 SG 3.82	The statutory guidance expects that health and safety issues should be covered in the 'assessment and training of foster carers', implying that this area should be covered in the preparation training provided to prospective carers.	
Safeguarding training for all foster carers equivalent to the basic level provided by LSCB	SG 3.84	Fostering services may want to consider making safeguarding training a part of their core programme.	
Safer carer training for foster carers, which addresses caring for children who have been abused	Standard 4.6 Standard 20.9	Standard 20.9 outlines how safer carer training should be offered to all members of the fostering household, not just foster carers, including young people when appropriate.	